ALL BOY

scrapbook pages

the growing up years

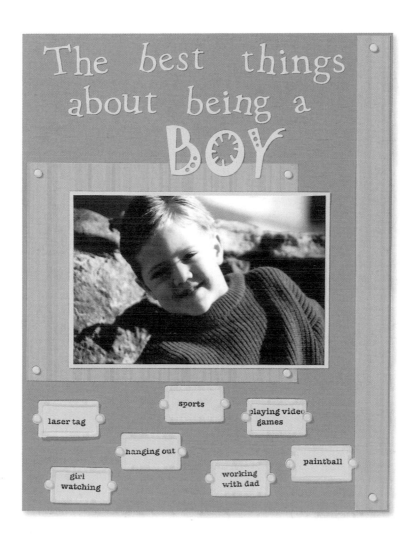

The best things about being a BOY

sports

laser tag

playing video games

hanging out

paintball

girl watching

working with dad

MEMORY MAKERS BOOKS

Executive Editor **Kerry Arquette**

Founder **Michele Gerbrandt**

Senior Editor **MaryJo Regier**

Art Director **Andrea Zocchi**

Designer **Nick Nyffeler**

Art Acquisitions Editor **Janetta Wieneke**

Craft Editor **Jodi Amidei**

Photographer **Ken Trujillo**

Contributing Photographers **Christina Dooley, Brenda Martinez, Jennifer Reeves**

Contributing Writer **Kelly Angard**

Contributing Artists **See Artist Index on page 110**

Editorial Support **Emily Curry Hitchingham, Dena Twinem**

Published by Memory Makers Books, an imprint of F & W Publications, Inc.
12365 Huron Street, Suite 500, Denver, CO 80234
Phone 1-800-254-9124
First edition. Printed in Singapore.

08 07 06 05 04 5432

A catalog record for this book is available from the U.S. Library of Congress

Distributed to trade and art markets by
F & W Publications, Inc.
4700 East Galbraith Road, Cincinnati, OH 45236
Phone 1-800-289-0963

ISBN 1-892127-34-2

Memory Makers is the home of *Memory Makers*, the scrapbook magazine dedicated to educating and inspiring scrapbookers. To subscribe, or for more information, call 1-800-366-6465. Visit us on the Internet at www.memorymakersmagazine.com.

This book belongs to

_____

We dedicate this book to all of our contributors who shared their
stunning boy scrapbook pages with us and to mothers everywhere
who may now be inspired to preserve cherished boyhood memories.

Table Of Contents

one

8-33 Attitude Is Everything

47 fresh page ideas to preserve a son's attitude—including everything from comical facial expressions and gut-busting giggles to big imaginations and outright orneriness

two

34-59 The Softer Side

49 innovative page ideas for capturing a boy's softer side— including everything from quiet contemplation and passionate wonderment to self-controlled gentleness and spontaneous tenderness

three

60-81 It's A Boy's Life

34 inspiring page ideas to help preserve a son's childhood enthusiasms—including everything from sporty competitiveness and satisfying the need for speed to musical giftedness and scouting

82-107 Boys Will Be Boys

46 captivating page ideas to help document boyhood antics—including everything from nature adventures and creature features to mud-wallowing and fixing or dismantling everything in sight

At eight years old, Daniel is crazy for Bionicles. He will spend hours creating his own creatures, making every combination he can come up with, each one having it's own character and unique style. On this day in early November, he had loads of fun showing off his creatures to both mom and for the camera.

Introduction

Raising a son is one of life's most wonderful experiences. It is a curious blend of discovery and diligence, marvel and mystery, pandemonium and patience, but most of all—joy!

It can also be one of the most challenging jobs a parent will ever have. Boys grow and change so fast it can be hard to keep up with them!

My son, Daniel, is no different. For him, I harbor great hopefulness and expectation for tomorrow, while flying by the seat of my pants today and trying to remember where yesterday went! His toddler years gave way to the grade school days, soon to be replaced by the oh-too-soon independent teen years—all in the blink of an eye! That's why it's so important to capture the fast-paced memories in the lives of our sons through photographic images and journaling.

All Boy Scrapbook Pages is created to help you seize and sanctify the marvel and mystery of the special boy in your life. Whether he's an airborne skateboarder or an eloquent musician, a sweet-smiling aristocrat or a tousle-haired ragamuffin who just dismantled his bike, you're sure to find inspiration in these poignant and outright adventurous layouts.

Celebrate the life and times of a son through scrapbook pages that capture the essence of boyhood and all the special rights of passage. With this book, I hope you will be inspired to preserve all of your son's winsome, entertaining, proud and rebellious moments. But get started soon; he will embark on adulthood before you know it!

You know, it really is true when they say there is a special bond between a mother and son.

Michele

Michele Gerbrandt
Founder
Memory Makers magazine

Supplies For Making Lasting Albums

The use of high-quality scrapbook materials will ensure cherished boyhood memories stay the course of time. We recommend the following:

- Archival-quality albums

- PVC free page protectors

- Acid- and lignin-free papers

- Acid-free and photo safe adhesives

- Pigment-ink pens and markers

- PVC-free memorabilia keepers, sleeves or envelopes

- Flat, photo-safe embellishments (encapsulate or place away from photos if questionable)

- De-acidifying spray for news clippings or documents

How To Make A Scrapbook Page
BUILD A PAGE FROM THE BACKGROUND OUT

Start with one to five photos for a single page. Gather any appropriate memorabilia. Select a background paper that pulls one color from your photos. Choose additional papers, based on colors in photos, if desired. Select or make page additions, if desired. Loosely assemble photos, title, journaling, memorabilia and page accents in desired layout for visual appeal. Trim and mat photos, mount in place with adhesive. Add title and journaling. Complete page with handmade or purchased page additions or accents. For instructions on how to replicate this page exactly, see page 110.

Attitude Is Everything

From the time of birth, boys are constantly developing new attitudes and behaviors while stretching the bounds of independence. Headstrong and unwavering, boys are clearly big spirits in little bodies, and throughout their growth spurts and testosterone surges, they learn that it's OK to abandon the "boy code" and just be themselves. Keep your camera close by during those special times when your son is exhibiting his attitude and his right to be different. From silly faces and gut-busting giggles to flexing muscles and running around buck-naked, boys need room to let their boldness breathe! As boys navigate the worlds of self-esteem and self-expression, they grow wings. Encourage expressive creativity and celebrate the diversity of masculinity. And most of all—love him for who he is.

It's not your aptitude but your attitude that will determine your altitude.

—*Jesse Jackson (adapted)*

Ryan, 11

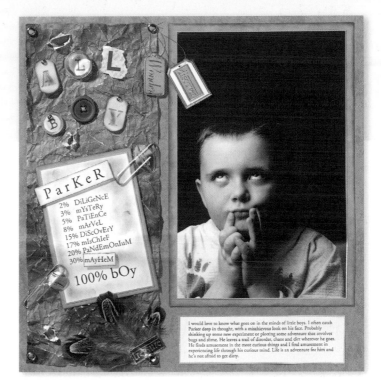

Parker

Shauna embraces the essence of a boy in curious contemplation with a random collection of collaged objects atop crumpled, sanded, torn and smudged paper. Cut patterned paper (Hot Off The Press, HOTP) to 4½ x 12"; crumple, flatten and sand. Tear small holes before vertically mounting at left side of brown paper with silver brads (Magic Scraps). Double mat photo on silver and green paper; brush edges of second mat with black chalk (Craf-T). Assemble title words from preprinted alphabet tiles (HOTP) cut and torn to size; mount on page with small silver brads (Magic Scraps). Mount large button (Magic Scraps) stitched with silver thread (DMC) as the letter "O." Embellish circle "tags" with silver embossing powder (PSX Design) and mount clear glass pebble (HOTP) over one letter. Adhere two silver word stickers (HOTP) to silver embossed tags; punch holes at top and string with silver thread. Dangle tags from brad at top of distressed border strip as shown. Print name, journaling and caption on white paper; cut to size and mat on silver and green paper. Smudge brown and black chalk on journaling block around text. Mount name and highlighted word to journaling block with self-adhesive foam spacers. Paper clip silver embossed sports-theme paper charms (HOTP) to border strip. Mount feathers (HOTP) at bottom right corner of border strip; adhere silver word (HOTP) over feathers as shown.

Shauna Berglund-Immel for Hot Off The Press, Canby, Oregon

Just Call Me J-Man

Kim reflects the big attitude of her little guy on a bold, color-blocked background. Cut patterned paper (SEI); mount on patterned paper background (SEI). Double mat photo on gray and white cardstock. Adhere letter stickers (SEI) on second mat and on background paper as shown.

Kim Haynes, Harrah, Oklahoma

Say Cheese

Polly contrasts photos of her son's silliness with elegant colors and a sophisticated layout. Tear two strips of patterned paper (Creative Imaginations); vertically mount at sides of patterned paper (Creative Imaginations) background. Cut photo corners from olive green cardstock. Mount photos on page; cut red satin ribbon (Offray) for photo corners. Cut title block and tag from red patterned paper (Lasting Impressions). Write title and name with black pen. Mat title block on red cardstock; tear bottom edge. Crop preprinted photo corners (Patchwork Paper Design); mount at corners of title block. Mat tag on red cardstock; tie with tan net (source unknown). Crop preprinted design (Patchwork Paper Design); mat on red cardstock and layer over netting wrapped around tag. Complete page with impressed wax seals (Papyrus) mounted on title block and tag.

Polly McMillan, Bullhead City, Arizona

Oh Boy, Oh Boy

Some boys make you laugh without even trying. Janett felt fortunate to have captured just one of her busy son's "gazillion goofy faces" on film and cleverly hid journaling about it beneath a title plate. Layer patterned paper (7 Gypsies) and colored cardstock strips to create background. Create black-and-white enlargement from color photo; mat and mount both on page. Computer-print journaling on lower half of cardstock; fold top over to create "card" and mount on page. Add title (Creative Imaginations) to front of journaling card. Stamp (source unknown) child's name and date to complete.

Janett McKee, Austin, Texas

Say Cheese!

Kim pokes some good, clean fun at her son's inability to smile sweetly for the camera in her journaling and selection of graphic design lines. Print title and journaling on blue background cardstock. Slice a 3¼" strip of patterned paper (Martha Stewart) and a 3¾" strip of orange cardstock. Horizontally layer and mount over light blue background cardstock. Double mat photo on solid cardstock; mount with small silver brad fasteners (Creative Impressions). Punch ¾", 1½" and 1¾" squares from solid and patterned papers. Layer and secure with small silver brads at bottom of page as shown.

Kim Haynes, Harrah, Oklahoma

My Boy

Kimberly captures the essence of her son during one of his sillier moments on brightly colored solid and patterned papers. Double mat large photo on orange and yellow cardstock. Layer on matted, patterned paper (Karen Foster Design). Print title, journaling and poem on solid and patterned (Paper Adventures) papers; trim to size and tear around edges. Crumple and flatten poem before mounting on lower left page. Double mat journaling on orange and yellow cardstock; mount atop matted patterned paper. Slice enlarged photo into six equal squares; reassemble at top of right page, leaving ⅛" between pieces. Double mat two photos together on patterned paper with printed title and orange cardstock.

Kimberly Lund, Wichita, Kansas

God Gave Us Faces...

Jlyne found a way to capture the many sides of her little boy's personality that is chock full of character. Mount enlarged and cropped photos on torn and ripped corrugated cardboard stained with walnut ink (7 Gypsies). Stamp photo captions and date under photos. Print journaling onto transparency; cut to size and mount at bottom of right page. Stain tag (source unknown) with walnut ink; stamp quote (Hero Arts) and tie with hemp string (Crafts Etc.).

Jlyne Hanback, Biloxi, Mississippi

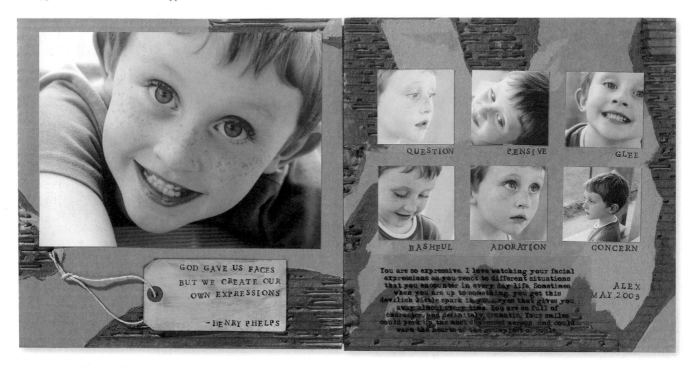

Making Faces

Maureen adds a bit of boyish charm to black-and-white photos and embellished tags with an attractive plaid fabric. Tear blue cardstock in half; mount vertically over tan cardstock background. Mat one photo on plaid fabric; embellish with buttons (Making Memories) along bottom edge of photo. Cut fabric into four ½" strips; frame photo mounted on blue torn cardstock with fabric strips. Mount rivets (Chatterbox) at corners. Crop ivory cardstock into tags; attach eyelets (Making Memories) and tie with fabric strips. Mount buttons along fabric strips, pen journaling and adhere title letter stickers (Creative Imaginations).

Maureen Spell, Carlsbad, New Mexico

Of All The Animals

Stephanie knew from the moment she took photos of her son running around and yelling like only little boys can do, she had the perfect page title to complement the photos. Mat photos on brown and light green cardstock before mounting on page. Attach brad fasteners just outside matting; frame matting with fuzzy fibers (EK Success). Slice a 4" strip of brown cardstock; mat on light green paper for title block. Print selected title words on green paper; mount one section on vellum tag (Making Memories) tied with fibers. Cut the others to size; tear top and bottom edges and brush with brown chalk. Mount silver tile letters (Creative Imaginations) and hang silver letter charms from fibers wrapped around title block. Trim preprinted wooden letter tiles (Hot Off The Press) to size; mount with self-adhesive foam spacers. Punch small photo square; mat on green paper tied with fibers.

Stephanie Ray, Little Rock, Arkansas

Keeper Of Our Hearts

Made for a special friend and her son, this layout preserves the boy's fun-loving attitude in a simple, uncluttered manner. First, machine-stitch netting down sides of cardstock and mount on cardstock to create background. Add cardstock strips across both pages for title; add child's name with letter eyelets (Making Memories) on one and embossed journaling on the other. Crop photos and set imprinted photo date aside, if applicable. Mat two photos. Mount photos on page, tucking partially beneath netting. Print character traits on vellum; tear and layer with a punched paper square atop metal tags (Making Memories). Add spiral clips (Making Memories) and hardware-store washers layered over cardstock circles. Finish with corner design—accent tiny manila envelope (FoofaLa) with chalk. Freehand cut and chalk vellum tag; tie together with metal-rimmed tag using fiber (EK Success). Adhere photo date imprint at center of metal tag.

Evana Willis, Huntley, New Zealand
Photos: Shanna Burkholder,
Monrovia, California

You Color Our World

Laura features her expressive son with a spectrum of colors for a simple yet dramatic layout. Mat photos on colored cardstocks; mount on black cardstock background. Cut colored cardstocks into 2" squares; mount in a horizontal row at the center of both pages. Print title on vellum; trim to size and tear all edges. Mount vellum title block over colored squares with brightly colored brads (Making Memories).

Laura Horowitz, Plantation, Florida

Brothers...Friends

Julie finds just the right words to describe not only the fun her two boys have together, but also the deep bond they share. Print title at bottom of light green cardstock; mat with yellow cardstock. Mount two photos on background. Print descriptive words in a variety of fonts on yellow cardstock; cut into strips and mount at left side of page as shown. Using a circle cutter (Creative Memories) or punches, cut four graduating circles from green, brown, pink, orange, blue and gray papers. Slice circles in halves, then in quarters; assemble into design as shown.

Julie Medeiros, Castle Rock, Colorado

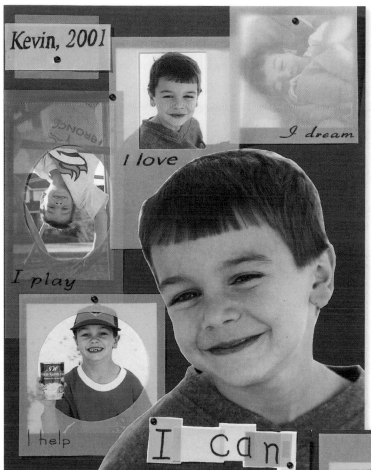

Kevin, 2001

I dream

I love

I play

I help

I can

I Can

Kelli focuses on the positive attributes of her son with shaped windows cut into softly colored vellum. Mount photos on black background cardstock. Using die cuts and a craft knife, cut window shapes into cropped pieces of colored vellum. Write descriptive journaling on vellum under cropped windows. Mount vellum over photos with black eyelets. Freehand cut vellum squares for title block; layer on white cardstock and trim. Write title with black pen and mount on page with black eyelets.

Kelli Noto, Centennial, Colorado

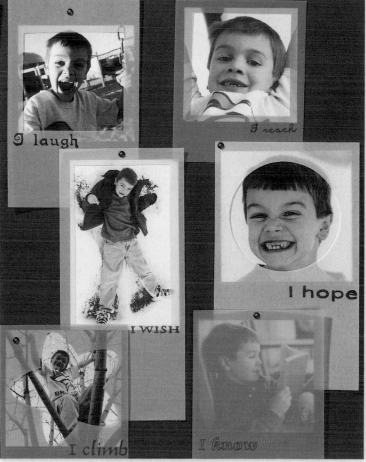

I laugh

I reach

I hope

I WISH

I climb

I know

Mitchell, 10

The journaling reads:

Jeramiah you have a wonderful imagination. You are always doing things that just make me laugh. You love to dress up like a cowboy, you have your own hat and real cowboy boots. You would wear them daily if I let you. One Saturday morning, you were wearing your pajamas, your boots and your hat. You were playing and I was on the computer. You said "Mom, look. I'm riding my horse." I thought to myself about what horse you could possibly be riding in the house. I turned around and laughed out loud at you as you rode the poor little horse all over. What an imaginative little boy I have.

Little Horse, Big Imagination

An imaginative little cowboy corrals his mom into riding along with him on the open range. Layer ivory speckled cardstock at top of left and bottom of right pages; crop circle in ivory cardstock as a window on right page. Print title and journaling on ivory cardstock. Tear edges around both; brush torn edges with brown and rust chalks (Craf-T). Attach copper eyelets (Making Memories) above and below title. Mat one photo on left page; cut photo corners from brown and ivory cardstocks for other photo. Tear one edge of ivory photo corners. Mat photo on right page over torn ivory cardstock strip brushed with chalk; attach eyelets at end of strip. Crop photo into circle; mount in circle-cut window next to journaling. Attach eyelets around circle window. Loop jute string through eyelets into design as shown. Brush around all eyelets with rust chalk for added interest.

Jennifer Cain, Highlands Ranch, Colorado

Kody, 10

Here Kitty-Kitty

Cheryl captures her young son's animalistic phase with simple finesse and a picture that speaks volumes. Computer-print title and journaling in text frames on background cardstock. Print clip art and animal sound on separate sheet of same-colored cardstock; trim and adhere. Mount photo to finish page.

Cheryl Overton, Kelowna, British Columbia, Canada

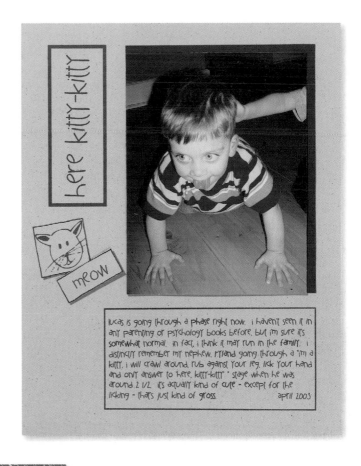

You Are So Ornery

Patterned papers covered with words emphasize the fact that Kim's son has no problem letting her know what's on his mind. Print partial title and journaling on brown cardstock. Slice a 2" strip of black patterned paper (7 Gypsies) and a 5" strip of burgundy cardstock; tear top and bottom edge. Layer burgundy cardstock with black patterned paper strip at top of brown cardstock. Mat two photos on patterned paper (7 Gypsies); layer with third photo on background. Adhere title letter rub-ons (Creative Imaginations) to silver brad fasteners (Creative Imaginations); mount brads above photo as shown. Tear small strip of black patterned paper; mount above journaling.

Kim Haynes, Harrah, Oklahoma

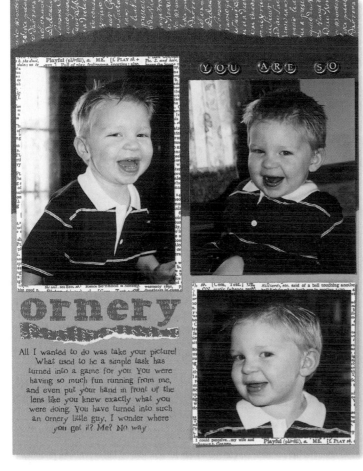

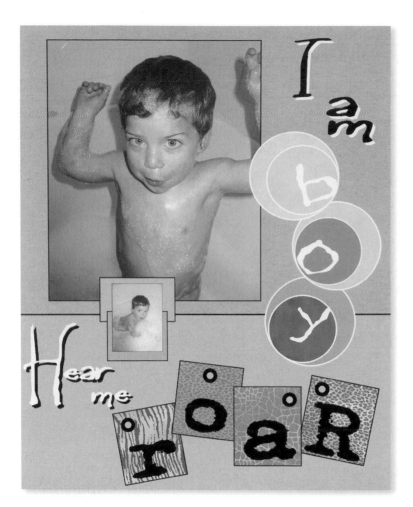

I Am Boy

Rhonda's son lets her know that he is King Of The Jungle with an earth-shattering roar. Re-create this computer-generated page (Scrapbook Factory Deluxe) by making a solid background; add color and texture to squares. Create circles; add color and texture. Scan animal-print papers. Make ring shapes; add black color for "eyelets." Layer title and journaling in desired fonts over shapes. To make page by hand, mount green cardstock at bottom of tan cardstock background. Slice thin strip of black cardstock; mount at top of green. Layer photos matted with cardstock over green and tan cardstock squares. Layer black and white letter stickers for part of title. Add white letter stickers to colored cardstock circles; mat on white cardstock and layer. Attach black letter stickers to animal print paper squares; add eyelets and layer at bottom of page.

Rhonda Altus, Walnut Grove, Missouri

Owie!

Funny how a bandage and a kiss from Mommy can turn a howling boy into a playful toddler. Re-create this computer generated page (Scrapbook Factory Deluxe) by adding colors and textures to background squares. Add colored stripes to white background. Scan patterned paper (7 Gypsies) for placeholder in layout; adhere actual paper over scanned image once finished with design. Use circle shapes and Roman numerals for clock. Duplicate small gray circles for chain. Make ring shapes metallic with illusion technique; fade white circles for tags' "vellum." Layer title and journaling in fonts of choice. To make page by hand, layer solid and patterned papers for color-blocked background. Mat photos and layer on background. Attach letter stickers at bottom for title. Write sentiment on vellum, metal-rimmed tags. Dangle from patterned paper strip with silver chain or fiber; mount patterned paper strip with self-adhesive foam spacers for depth. Stamp clock on vellum, crop and mount as shown.

Rhonda Altus, Walnut Grove, Missouri

Glimpses

Rhonda likens taking photos of her son to "trying to stand on the ground in the middle of a tornado!" Re-create this computer-generated page (Scrapbook Factory Deluxe) with colored stripes on white background. Add color to a square. Layer sized color and black-and-white photos. Use illusion technique on circles for title. Use various shapes and techniques to create "bookplate." Layer title and date in fonts of choice. To make page by hand, start with striped patterned paper mounted at the top and bottom of green cardstock. Mat photos on black cardstock; layer cropped photos along the top of page. Print part of title on vellum and tan cardstock; attach letter pebbles or round metal letter eyelets for word "faces." Cut name on tan cardstock to fit behind metal bookplate; mount at bottom of title block. Complete title with black letter stickers adhered above vellum block.

Rhonda Altus, Walnut Grove, Missouri

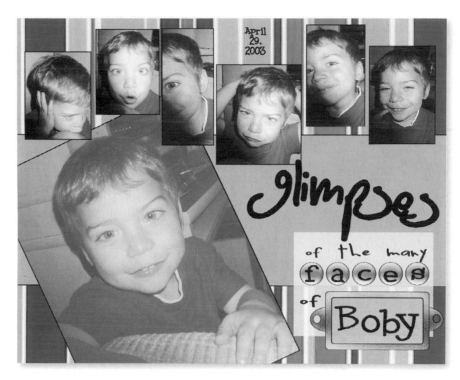

All Boy

Renae keeps the focus of her page on the exuberant energy of three silly boys with a simple layout and minimal embellishments. Slice two ¾" strips of black cardstock. Slice one ½" and one 4" strip of patterned paper (source unknown). Layer black strips over patterned paper at top and bottom of turquoise cardstock as shown. Attach white flat eyelets (Making Memories) at ends of black strips. Punch two 1" and 1¼" squares from gray and black cardstock; adhere word stickers (Creative Imaginations) on layered squares. Crop gray cardstock into tag shape; mat with black cardstock and trim. Layer two ¾" strips of solid and patterned papers on tag. Adhere sticker sentiment (Creative Imaginations); mount on page with white flat eyelet.

Renae Clark, Mazomanie, Wisconsin

Static

Cheryl preserves a favorite playtime activity in a simple, electrifying display that keeps your eyes focused on the photos. Computer-generate or hand print journaling along lower edge of cardstock background. Mount a block of complementary-colored cardstock on background. Add computer- or hand-printed title on page and mount photos. Finish with pen stroke details in black ink.

Cheryl Overton, Kelowna, British Columbia, Canada

A Little Bit Of Spike

A new haircut can do wonders for how we feel about ourselves...but in this case, Kim's son already had the spunky attitude and then got the haircut to match! Mat patterned paper (Magenta) on red cardstock; mount large eyelets (Creative Imaginations) at corners. Crop photos into equal-sized squares; mount on taupe cardstock. Print title on vellum; cut to size and double mat with patterned and solid papers. Mount on taupe cardstock with small eyelets (Making Memories). Write journaling on vellum with black pen; mount on page with small eyelets.

Kim Haynes, Harrah, Oklahoma

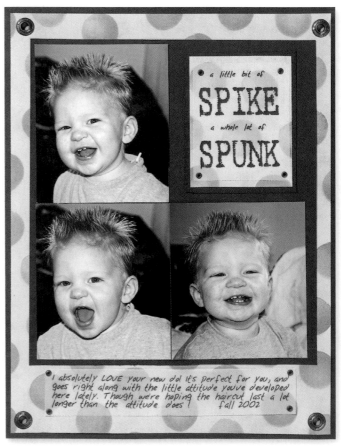

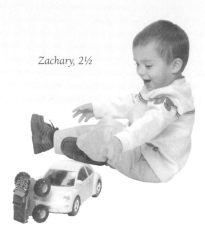

Zachary, 2½

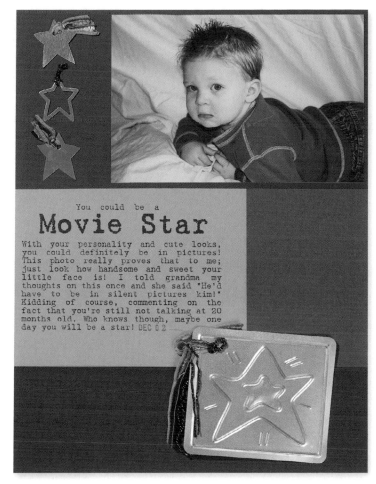

Movie Star

Kim features her shining star with sparkling silver accents. Print title and journaling on mustard cardstock. Slice a 3" strip of rust cardstock; vertically mount at right side of page. Slice a 4¼" and a 2½" strip of brown cardstock; horizontally mount at top and bottom of page with photo as shown. Tie small and large metal stars (Making Memories) with fibers (source unknown); mount at left of photo and at bottom of page. Stamp date (Avery) at end of journaling with brown ink.

Kim Haynes, Harrah, Oklahoma

Wild Thing

Animal print paper and tied raffia lends a thematic element to Hilary's wild-haired boy. Double mat photo on dark green and tan cardstocks. Print title and journaling on white cardstock; trim to size. Layer photo, title and journaling on patterned paper (Frances Meyer). Tie raffia into a small bunch; mount at right of photo. Tie three knots into jute string; mount at bottom of page.

Hilary Erickson, Santa Clara, California

Picky Eater

Kim adds interest to a list of her son's food likes and dislikes with black eyelets. Print lists on brown cardstock; attach eyelets to highlight items. Print partial title and journaling on rust cardstock; tear bottom edge and mount atop brown cardstock background. Mat photos on black cardstock. Adhere letter stickers (Wordsworth) to patterned paper (Treehouse Designs); cut to size. Mat two letters on rust cardstock before mounting on page. Layer torn rust cardstock over cropped patterned paper at bottom right corner as shown.

Kim Haynes, Harrah, Oklahoma

Baby You Can Eat Crackers

Rhonda's son clearly states his preference as to where he likes to enjoy his favorite snack. Re-create this computer-generated page (Scrapbook Factory Deluxe) by "detinting" a color photo, leaving just the product in color. Make a gray square background. Color circles black and gold beneath some title letters. Layer title and date in desired fonts. To make page by hand, start with a strip of gray cardstock vertically mounted on white cardstock next to an enlarged photo. Either hand tint photo, or layer a silhouette-cropped photo atop a black-and-white reprint for same effect. Adhere letter stickers or write title on small colored tags or punched cardstock circles. Write date at bottom of page with black pen.

Rhonda Altus, Walnut Grove, Missouri

Your Giggle

Christina ties in the title of her page with a subtle patterned paper and a photo that speaks volumes. Mount photo on tan background cardstock. Cut 3½" and 2½" squares from tan cardstock; diagonally tear and brush edges with brown chalk before mounting at photo's corners as shown. Slice a 4¼" piece of patterned paper (Amscan); vertically mount at right side of layout. Horizontally mount fibers (EK Success), securing at back of page. Write title on tan cardstock; cut to size and tear edges. Brush edges with brown chalk and mount to page with self-adhesive foam spacers.

Christina Chrushch, Rocky Mount, North Carolina

Laugh

Nothing brings a smile to a mother's face quicker than the sound of her child laughing. Kim captured her son in such a moment and highlights his delightful face with a colorful and artistic patterned paper. Slice a 4¼" strip of patterned paper (Wordsworth); vertically mount over black background cardstock. Mat photo on vellum; layer over background. Adhere letter stickers (Wordsworth) on silver-rimmed vellum tags (Making Memories); mount to page with small black brads over patterned paper strips.

Kim Haynes, Harrah, Oklahoma

Playground Warriors

Renae assembles a collection of metal and letter stickers for a title as wild and creative as her playful "warriors." Layer a 9½ x 12" piece of white cardstock with a 2" strip of mesh (Magic Mesh) on blue cardstock. Slice two ½" pieces of yellow cardstock and one ½" piece of black cardstock; horizontally mount at top and bottom of page as shown. Mount black and blue brads (Making Memories) at ends of strips. Double mat large photo on yellow and black cardstocks. Mount silver tags (Chronicle Books) on second mat with small silver brads. Print journaling on vellum; layer over double-matted photo and attach silver brads (Making Memories) at corners. Assemble title from an assortment of different letter stickers (EK Success, Making Memories) adhered on silver-rimmed tags (Making Memories) and paper scraps with circle clip, metal letters (Making Memories) and letters cut from preprinted paper (Hot Off The Press). Mount on mesh layered over blue and black cardstocks; attach small silver brads at lower corners.

Renae Clark, Mazomanie, Wisconsin

The Fun Never Stops

Virginia's quick and easy layout reflects the simple joy her little boy experienced when playing with a new ball. Mat photo on a large strip of blue paper; tear right edge and mount on patterned background paper (SEI). Adhere sticker title (EK Success) at top of photo mat. Mount silver-rimmed tags (Making Memories) to background with small silver brads (Creative Impressions). Write journaling on tags with blue pen.

Virginia Haverick, Nutley, New Jersey

Carefree Personality

Chanelle's son gives true meaning to "don't worry, be happy" with his joyful and carefree personality. Using two-sided tape or clear-drying glue, mount fibers around two pieces of blue cardstock for a colorful border. Mat one photo on yellow cardstock; mount all photos on pages. Cut title letters from blue cardstock using template (Scrap Pagerz); mount on white cardstock strip. Attach white square eyelet (Making Memories) to one letter and wooden firefly (Provo Craft) on another. Complete title with silver word tag (Chronicle Books) tied with thin strip of blue paper. Print journaling on white cardstock; cut to size and mount. Mount square buttons above journaling block and on blue cardstock strip matted with white cardstock. Add pen details to title and journaling blocks, as well as decorative button strips. Complete scrapbook page with white "rub-on" descriptive words (Making Memories) and wooden fireflies (Provo Craft).

Chanelle Nesmith, Marietta, Georgia

Mitchell, 10

Accessorizing Boys

Oksanna captures her son's love of bugs with humor alongside an enlarged photo showcasing a long-legged friend. Print journaling on cream cardstock; layer with light and dark blue cardstock squares atop patterned paper (Design Originals). Mat photo on brown cardstock; mount under journaling. Fold back lower right corner of cream cardstock and adhere; embellish with metallic dimensional paint (Duncan) and stitched button (EK Success). Stamp partial title (All Night Media) on cream and brown cardstocks with black ink. Die cut large title word from gold metallic paper (DMD); mat on brown cardstock and trim.

Oksanna Pope, Los Gatos, California

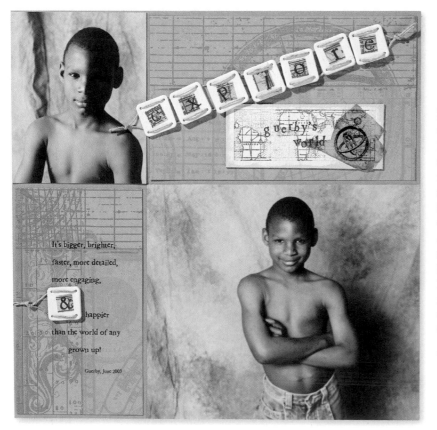

Explore

Elizabeth documents her son's philosophical view of life and the world around him. Divide blue cardstock into quadrants; crop and enlarge photos to fit two quadrants. Print journaling on patterned cardstock (Club Scrap); crop to fit quadrants. Stamp map (Club Scrap) and part of title (PSX Design) on matte board; cut to size. Adhere sticker (Club Scrap) on mica tile scrap (USArtQuest); mount on matte board. Adhere title letter stickers (Creative Imaginations) on small squares punched from patterned paper (Club Scrap); layer on tiny tiles (Sweetwater). Link tiles together with hemp string.

Elizabeth Ruuska, Rensselaer, Indiana

Boys Will Be Boys

Jaimie unites random photos of her boys with a classic parental admonition. Mount a 1½" strip of patterned paper (Karen Foster Design) to create left border. Crop, mat and mount three standard photos as shown. To create title, adhere letter stickers (EK Success, Provo Craft) on cardstock, tear edges and chalk with brown. Mat torn title pieces with additional torn cardstock; mount "Boys" on fourth mat. Mount the rest of the title on freehand-cut and torn tag. Create two additional freehand-cut and torn tags; add matted photos. Tie fibers (Rubba Dub Dub) on all tags; layer and mount on page to finish.

Jaimie Rivale, St. Charles, Missouri

Sob, Cry

Janett seizes the moment of her son's tears over not getting any more catsup to eat with humor and wisdom. Start adding blocks of cardstock and patterned paper (American Crafts) on background for visual appeal. Mount punched 1¼" squares on background as shown; top upper set with letter stickers (Creative Imaginations) and lower set with letter eyelets (Making Memories). Add spiral clip to fiber (EK Success) and string across lower border; adhere on back of page and atop punched square. Mount photos, one matted, and add metal photo corners (Making Memories). Computer-print journaling; trim and adhere.

Janett McKee, Austin, Texas

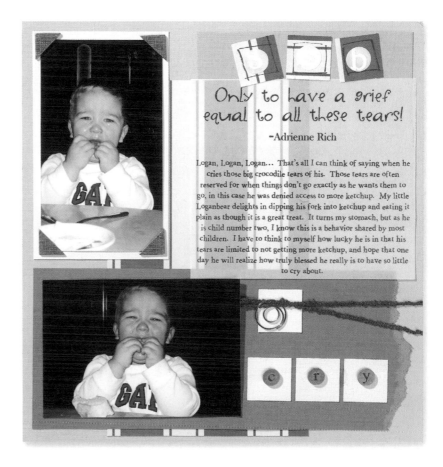

Soul Of
A Poet

Tina pays tribute to the "thoughtful" side of her son with a muted computer-generated layout (Microsoft Digital Image Pro). To create page digitally, scan photo or download digital photo and size. Overlay title atop photo with a transparent background. Add black journaling block with white text in desired font. To re-create this same look by hand, start with an enlarged black-and-white photo mounted on white cardstock. Cut title letters and heart from vellum or adhere vellum letter stickers. Print journaling in reverse or write with a white gel pen on black cardstock. Horizontally mount under photo as shown.

Tina Chambers, Sardinia, Ohio

Time Keeps
On Slipping

Janice's photography-class photo of her son at age 3—lit only by a desk lamp—inspired a second photo, using the same lighting, of her son at 18 for a striking "then and now" comparison. To create digitally (Adobe Photoshop 7.0), set background to black and layer the two photos; add white stroke mat. Rotate, skew, size, adjust opacity for transparency and tint blue several variations of clip art pocket watch (Hemera) images; layer and merge onto black background. Add white title blocks with shape tool; overlay duplicated title word, rotating one layer. To create page by hand, layer watch art (stamped, photo-cropped, paper or sticker watches) onto black background. Mat photos on white, layer on page. Add punched white squares for title. Adhere template-cut or letter stickers to complete title and journaling.

Janice Dye-Szucs, Markham, Ontario, Canada

Justin Thomas

A little boy's serious side is complemented with descriptive words and spiral clip embellishments. Print title on white cardstock; mat enlarged photo on cardstock. Mount over black cardstock layered with white drywall tape. Print descriptive words on white cardstock; trim to size. Secure word strips to photo mat with circle clips (Making Memories). Vertically mount white fibers along left side of photo mat.

Angela Marvel, Puyallup, Washington

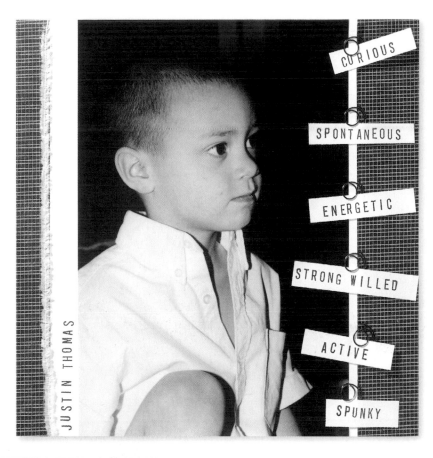

Picture Perfect

Kim highlights the softer side of her son with pastel colored strips offset by a dramatic black background. Double mat photo on light orange and black cardstocks. Layer over strips cut from patterned paper (KI Memories) mounted to black cardstock with small black and copper brad fasteners (Karen Foster Design). Adhere letter stickers (Creative Imaginations) to pre-printed accent squares (KI Memories). Slice a ¾" strip of vellum; mount to page over accent squares with small black brad fasteners. Write balance of title on vellum.

Kim Haynes, Harrah, Oklahoma

Silly Face

Silly faces run the gamut from being cute and funny to mean and silly snarls as Jennifer illustrates with a photo of her son in rare form. Print journaling on yellow cardstock; slice into a 3" strip and mount near top of navy blue cardstock background. Slice two ½" strips and one 1½" strip of patterned cardstock (Bo Bunny Press); horizontally mount ½" strips above and below yellow cardstock and 1½" strip at bottom of page. Slice a ¼" strip of white cardstock; brush edges with navy blue chalk and mount above patterned strip at bottom of page. Print title on white cardstock; silhouette and brush edges with navy blue chalk before mounting at top of page. Slice navy blue and yellow strips of cardstock in random widths; mount on white cardstock for photo mat. Triple mat photo on yellow and striped cardstocks. Punch ¾" and 1" circles from yellow cardstock; mount atop white cardstock strip. Attach mini navy blue buttons (Hero Arts) on ¾" circles.

Jennifer Bourgeault,
Macomb Township, Michigan

Silly

Angela knows that even though there's never of shortage of silly faces to take pictures of, she had to capture her son's funny face to remember the carefree days of his childhood. Layer an 11¼" square of blue cardstock slightly askew over dark blue cardstock. Attach silver letter charms (Making Memories) with blue eyelets at top of background. Print quote on blue cardstock; trim to 9¾ x 7½" and mat on darker blue cardstock. Attach eyelets at corners; weave fibers (Fibers By The Yard) through eyelets to frame matting. Mount photo next to quote with silver photo corners (Making Memories).

Angela Marvel, Puyallup, Washington

Jake, 6

Boy, Tough, Grit

Miley's son may look like a tough guy, but wash away the dirt, and his sweet face reappears. Add texture to blue background paper: spray with water, crumple, flatten and iron. Tear a hole at middle of page; gently curl edges away from tear. Mount flat eyelets (Making Memories) at opposite corners as shown. Slice a 3¼" strip of brown cardstock; vertically mount at left side of page. Print title and definition on brown cardstock; cut title words to size and mat on blue cardstock. Mount fibers (source unknown) along right side of brown cardstock strip. Adhere definition to back of page, exposing words through torn, curled hole in page. Mount matted title words on small tags (DMD) brushed with brown chalk. Mount small buttons stitched with fibers at right of title tags; attach flat eyelets on tags. Mat photo on brown cardstock; mount button stitched with fibers along two sides of matted photo. Mount three buttons and fibers at bottom of page in design as shown; attach flat eyelets at ends of fibers. Stamp date (source unknown) on brown cardstock; cut to size and mat.

Miley Johnson, Omaha, Nebraska

Want A Piece Of Me?

Renee gives in to the old adage "boys will be boys" whenever her boys decide to turn the living room into a wrestling ring. Diagonally layer an 8½ x 11" piece of red cardstock over blue cardstock. Horizontally mount gingham ribbon near bottom of page. Mat large photo with tan cardstock. Slice a 4 x 6½" window into a 5 x 7" piece of tan cardstock; tilt photo and secure upper left and lower right corners beneath inside of window frame as shown. Print journaling on tan cardstock, leaving room for small photo matted on red cardstock at center of journaling. Mat on blue cardstock. Print highlighted word of title on red cardstock and cut with a craft knife; print remainder of title and assemble as shown. Embellish journaling block with gingham ribbon and double mat with blue and tan cardstocks.

Renee Villalobos-Campa, Winnebago, Illinois

Liam Is All Boy

Evana documents the adventures of a busy boy with a monochromatic page layered with dimensional details. Tear two 1" strips of patterned paper (7 Gypsies); brush edges with brown chalk. Mount at top and bottom of brown matted cardstock over vertically mounted brown tulle. Single and triple mat photos; layer on top of and below tulle as shown. Print part of title and journaling on vellum; cut to size and tear top and bottom edges. Brush torn edges with brown chalk and add pen detail. Snip off tops of silver metal letters (Making Memories); press on embossing pad and sprinkle with clear embossing powder. Set with heat gun. Layer torn cardstock, photo scraps and patterned paper atop silver-rimmed tags (Making Memories). Mount embossed metal letters with torn vellum pieces brushed with brown chalk on layered tags. Attach silver brad fastener on vellum title strip with fibers (EK Success); mount tags atop fibers.

Evana Willis, Huntley, New Zealand

Are We Cool Or What?

Susan's boys in blue jeans show off confident attitudes with the strike of a cool pose. Print partial title and journaling on brown cardstock. Tear ½" and 4" strips of patterned paper (Colorbök); horizontally mount at center and bottom of brown cardstock. Adhere border sticker (Magenta) above torn strip at bottom of page. Machine or hand stitch around cardstock ¼" from edges. Double mat photos on white and navy cardstocks; tear bottom edge of first mat. Cut title letters using template (source unknown) from patterned paper. Complete page with small brad fasteners (Making Memories) around title.

Susan Stringfellow, Cypress, Texas

Dennis The Menace

Shannon documents her son's strong comparison to a charming yet curious cartoon character, *Dennis the Menace®*. Double mat photos on green and dark brown cardstocks. Print journaling on tan cardstock and double mat. Cut title letters using template (EK Success) from green cardstock; mat on black cardstock and trim. Write balance of title on green cardstock; mat with black cardstock. Spray newspaper cartoon with an archival preservation treatment (EK Success); mat on black cardstock. Mount photos, journaling, cartoon and title on patterned paper (Frances Meyer).

Shannon Taylor, Bristol, Tennessee

All About Aaron

No amount of dirt and grime can erode the confidence of Melissa's 5-year-old son. Cut a 6½" piece of patterned paper (Karen Foster Design); diagonally mount on dark green cardstock. Trim off corners with scissors. Print lists on vellum; cut to size and layer on page. Attach eyelets at top of one journaling block and at corners of the other. Layer patterned paper triangle over vellum square; attach large eyelet at center. Loop hemp string through eyelets to look like journaling block is hanging on page.

Melissa Brown, Fort Walton Beach, Florida

The Softer Side

Filled with passion and wonder, boys can be disarming in their times of gentleness and self-control. Be on the lookout for those elusive boyhood moments when "the softer side" shows itself—that sudden and unpredictable transformation from boundless energy to quiet contemplation; those times when little heroes and warriors melt your heart and touch your soul with their spontaneous tenderness. Watch your son when he closes his eyes to dream and think long, long thoughts. With your camera in hand, capture his body language. Hear his sounds of silence. See with both ears and listen with both eyes. You will be rewarded with emotional insight as your son explores his oneness, separateness and interdependence with family, friends and the world around him. Shhhh...

John, 8

When the heart speaks, the tongue is silent.
—Author unknown

A Smile So Sweet

Cheryl showcases tender photos of her son's sweet smile in monochromatic colors pulled from the boy's sweater. Computer-print title in font of choice on green cardstock; tear edge and mount on black background. Mat enlarged and cropped photos on torn green cardstock; adhere. Finish page with sage green fiber wrapped around lower end of page; secure on back with tape.

Cheryl Overton, Kelowna, British Columbia, Canada

Love

A tender moment between brothers is enhanced with distressed paper and hand-stitched details. Crumple and flatten tan and burgundy cardstocks; mat tan cardstock on burgundy cardstock. Loosely stitch cardstocks together with brown embroidery floss. Tear edges of distressed burgundy cardstock; mat enlarged photo. Curl edges in toward photo using fingers before mounting on tan cardstock. Cut preprinted design elements (EK Success); mount along bottom of page. Create stitched lettering; write names with pencil or chalk on tan cardstock. Using a paper-piercing tool or a sewing needle, punch small holes to be stitched; erase pencil or chalk. Stitch names using brown embroidery thread. Complete page using journaling details with a black pen.

Renee Villalobos-Campa, Winnebago, Illinois

Jackson

Mary Anne journals a special message to her son detailing his unique characteristics. Print name, title letters, journaling and quote on patterned paper (Wordsworth). Cut quote strip to size and mount near top of matted patterned paper (Wordsworth); attach gold eyelets at corners. Mat both photos on black cardstock. Tear all edges of large photo mat; press torn edges on Versamark pad (Tsukineko). Sprinkle with gold ultra thick embossing enamel; melt with heat gun, aiming hot air toward photo so that UTEE (Ranger) melts onto photo. Using a craft knife and ruler, slice a frame around photo on three sides to make flip-up window shown below. Mat on black cardstock; stamp word (PSX Design) at bottom of photo. Crop printed title letters on patterned paper into squares with decorative scissors; mount on black cardstock. Add gold dot design to letter squares with gold leaf pen. Layer and mount letters along bottom edge of embossed matted photo. Stamp clock (Inkadinkado) with gold ink on black cardstock; sprinkle with UTEE and set with a heat gun. Silhouette cut image and mount on matted photo. Create flip-up photo with hidden journaling; cut journaling to size. Trim right side into decorative shape using a template or decorative ruler; mat on black cardstock cut to the same size as matted photo. Attach hinge to matted photo and journaling with gold eyelets as shown. Silhouette-cut title and vertically mount on left side of page.

Mary Anne Walters, Ramsdell, Tadley, England

You Are My Dandelion Wish

A mother's heart is warmed when her son stops to pluck a few dandelions and present them to her. Mat photos on white cardstock; layer on patterned paper (Paper Adventures). Print some title words on vellum; trim to size and mount at top of page. Crop circles from patterned paper; adhere letter and number stickers (Doodlebug Design).

Renee Villalobos-Campa, Winnebago, Illinois

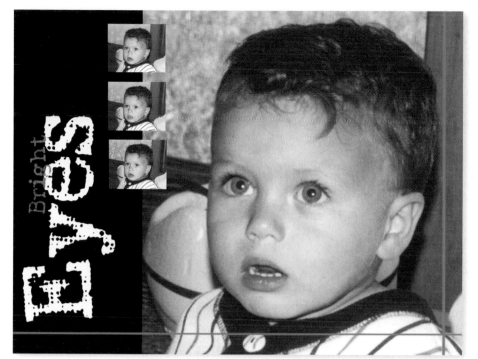

Bright Eyes

Amy captures wide-eyed innocence with just a hint of color in a computer-generated layout (Adobe Photoshop). Scan or download image; duplicate tiny image three times. Tint eyes blue in photo enlargement. Layer photos on black background. Add title in font of choice. To re-create this layout by hand, slice a strip of black cardstock; vertically mount next to enlarged photo. Hand tint black-and-white photo. Crop or punch small photos; layer over photo and border strip. Adhere letter stickers for title.

Amy Alvis, Indianapolis, Indiana

Quiet Thoughts

A rare moment of calm in the eye of a storm is captured by Janett and shared through simple design and successful focus. Layer cropped and torn patterned papers (7 Gypsies, Mustard Moon) over patterned background (SEI) and adhere. Flatten paper yarn (Making Memories) and stamp title; wrap around photos and mount on page. Complete page with poem stones (Creative Imaginations) along right border on background paper.

Janett McKee, Austin, Texas

Always Watching Over You

Wanda uses an enlarged image softened under a vellum overlay to express her deep love and sense of responsibility for her son. Mount enlarged photo on black cardstock; mount vellum over matted photo with small blue brad fasteners (Limited Edition Rubberstamps). Mat photo on black cardstock; mount over vellum. Adhere letter stickers (Creative Imaginations, Provo Craft) to vellum strip; mount on page with small black brad fasteners (Limited Edition Rubberstamps).

Wanda Santiago-Cintron, Deerfield, Wisconsin

These Hands Of Yours

Jane illustrates that even small hands can say and do so much. Mat photo on white cardstock; mount on patterned paper (SEI). Print title on vellum; cut to size and mount on page over torn white cardstock. Attach with square brad fasteners (Making Memories). Enhance layout with descriptive words: stamp words (PSX Design) on vellum silver-rimmed tag (Making Memories) and green cardstock. Mount tag with silver eyelet and green cardstock with self-adhesive foam spacers. Print words on blue paper, taupe cardstock and vellum. Cut all to size; brush edges of blue torn paper with blue chalk. Mount glass pebble (Making Memories) over first letter. Attach vellum with silver square and white eyelets (Making Memories). Add chalk and pen detail to taupe cardstock; mount on page with self-adhesive foam spacers. Mount silver word charm beneath title. Attach silver letters (Making Memories) with small silver brads (Making Memories).

Jane Hasty, Chicago, Illinois

Son

Ralonda acknowledges how fast her oldest child is growing up with a lovely poem about "letting go." Slice a ½" and a 2¾" strip of patterned paper (Paper Adventures). Slice a ½" and a 1" strip of black cardstock. Horizontally layer black cardstock and patterned paper at top and bottom of olive green cardstock as shown. Print poem on transparency (3M); cut to size and mount at left side of page, securing ends under black cardstock strips. Mount photos and quote charm (Making Memories) at right of poem. Add black color to silver metal letters (Making Memories) with a specialty pen (American Crafts) before mounting near bottom of page.

Ralonda Heston, Murfreesboro, Tennessee

My Beautiful Boy

Alex creates a soft, monochromatic design in shades of blue as a background for a sweet photo of her baby boy. Run brayer and stamp ink pads on white background in various shades of blue, layering colors for dimension and depth. Finish by stamping shadow stamps in coordinating colors. Mat photo with blue cardstock; adhere. Stamp title (source unknown) with blue ink.

Alex Bishop, Bountiful, Utah

Zachary, 2½

Take Time To Smell The Roses

Shandy features a timeless saying and showcases hand-tinted photos of her boys during extraordinarily peaceful moments in the yard. Use solid-colored cardstock to color block the background of a page spread. Add a bar of punched and matted 1" squares on left page. Crop and mat photos, assemble with one additional punched square across pages for visual appeal. Computer-print title and journaling on vellum and tear edges. Mount journaling on pages using eyelets. Finish spread with eyelet letters (Making Memories) to spell out "roses;" attach with brad fasteners.

Shandy Vogt, Nampa, Idaho

It's The Little Things

Vanessa captures a rare moment of peace and quiet from her wild and crazy 3-year-old. Embellish preprinted embossed paper (All My Memories) with cropped preprinted designs (EK Success) at left side of left page and bottom of right page; layer elements on patterned paper with torn edges and brown cardstock. Mat three photos on patterned paper (source unknown); tear one edge of two mats. Layer cropped preprinted photo corners on two photos. Slice a 1¼" strip of brown cardstock; vertically mount on left page. Punch 1" squares of patterned paper; mount atop cardstock strip. Layer preprinted design on cardstock strip; stitch to page with embroidery thread. Add crisscross stitching at bottom of photos on left and right page with embroidery thread. Print title on brown cardstock; cut to size. Stamp name, date and quote (Colorbök, Plaid) on brown cardstock; cut to size. Tear bottom edge of cardstock with name and date. Layer title with cropped preprinted designs and patterned paper squares at top of right page. Complete page with wire details; pierce small holes and thread wire through holes creating designs as shown.

Vanessa Spady, Virginia Beach, Virginia

Maclain

Elizabeth celebrates the unique personality and marvelous mind of her son with an artistic portrait and touching story. Quadruple mat photo on brown and rust cardstocks and patterned paper (Club Scrap). Mount cropped photos behind metal frames (Making Memories); layer at left side of brown cardstock background. Tie hemp cord to charms and bottle (7 Gypsies) filled with micro beads (Ranger). Attach to circle clip (7 Gypsies); mount at side of photo mat. Cut a 9" piece of netting (Scrappin' Fools); fold over each end two times, creating a pocket with enforced sides. Attach to page with small silver brads. Print journaling on patterned cardstock (Club Scrap). Crop text into equal-sized tags; punch and re-punch circle at top of tag. Loop metal chain (American Tag Co.) through tags and mesh pocket. Stamp name on green paper; crop to fit behind bookplate (source unknown). Cut mini tag from watercolor paper; write date with black pen. Stain small tag and name with walnut ink; mount name behind bookplate. Attach small tag to bookplate with small silver brads.

Elizabeth Ruuska, Rensselaer, Indiana

Owen

Chris shows the rapid transition from baby to big boy with photos on a destination-themed layout. Mat photo on blue cardstock; tear all edges. Wrap fibers (source unknown) around bottom of photo mat; mount on patterned paper background (Club Scrap) with self-adhesive foam spacers. Mount compass on small tag (both Leave Memories); attach to photo mat with spiral clip (source unknown). Mount small photo under metal frame (Making Memories) at bottom of page. Glue glass pebble over "I love you" sentiment (Leave Memories) at lower right photo mat corner. Stamp title (Hampton Art) with black ink and print journaling on transparency; cut to size. Stamp date (Staples) with brown ink.

Chris Sullivant, Nashville, Tennessee

Wonderment

Kenna knows it would be hard to guess the many things that go through her child's mind, so she settles for a few photos of her son lost in thought. Mat gray patterned paper (Mustard Moon) on blue cardstock for both pages. Slice a 3" strip of blue patterned paper (Mustard Moon); vertically mount on left page. Slice a 6½" piece of gray patterned paper (Mustard Moon); mount on right page. Silhouette denim overall photo image (Creative Imaginations); mount at left side of left page. Quadruple mat large photo on solid and patterned papers. Mount square eyelets (Making Memories) at corners of third matting before mounting on page. Print title on vellum; trim to size and mount sideways next to silhouette-cut photo image. Horizontally and vertically mount fibers (Fibers By The Yard) on right page as shown. Mat large photo on blue patterned paper; attach silver eyelets on matting. String letter beads (Westrim) on blue embroidery thread; feed through eyelets and secure at back of page. Mount stitched buttons (Making Memories) and square eyelets under matted photo. Cut photo image scraps into strips; diagonally mount on corners of last photo. Adhere quote sticker (Wordsworth) to complete page.

Kenna Ewing, Parkside, Pennsylvania

Kody & Kameron, 10 & 6

Little Boys' Pockets Hold

Jessica's son wears the frosting from his cupcake almost as sweetly as a pair of comfortable overalls. Machine stitch around edges of blue cardstock pages, allowing stitches to be skipped and ragged for a rougher look. Mat two photos on tan cardstock; cut photo corners from tan cardstock and mount on one matted photo. Stitch around edges of matting. Layer preprinted paper hat accent (EK Success) over torn blue cardstock stitched on tan cardstock. Slice ½" strips of tan cardstock; write and stamp (PSX Design) select words of poem. Write balance of poem words with white pencil (EK Success) on background. Stamp date (Staples) at side of photo.

Jessica Harvey, Bucksport, Maine

Enamor

Tenika's son is intensely interested in nature's sights and sounds and quite fascinated with the environment around him. Diagonally layer sheer printed ribbon across photo mounted on patterned paper (Chatterbox). Adhere letter stickers (SEI) and dragonfly sticker (Colorbök) near top of page. Mount silver preprinted circle embellishments (KI Memories) to the right of title stickers. Write journaling at bottom of page with black pen.

Tenika Morrison, Puyallup, Washington

Onederful

Cheryl takes her cue from the soft colors and clean, simple lines in the photo of her son for her layout. Mat enlarged photo on ivory cardstock; mount over yellow vellum and blue mesh (Magenta) strips with torn ends mounted on green cardstock. Print title and journaling on vellum; cut to size and tear top and bottom edges. Mount over right side of matted photo. Attach metal number eyelet (Making Memories) over blue mesh scrap.

Cheryl Pulla, Whitby, Ontario, Canada

Peek

Michele emphasizes the curious nature of her little boy with a cropped photo that gives the illusion that his face is coming through the page. Crop photo; layer with patterned paper (Chatterbox) over brown cardstock. Print title on orange cardstock; silhouette and mount at bottom of page. Finish with handwriten journaling on patterned paper.

Michele Woods, Worthington, Ohio

Hunter

Certain photos stand alone in a mother's heart, bringing a realization that her baby is growing up way too fast. Double mat photo on patterned paper (Design Originals) and brown cardstock. Free-hand or die cut letter "H" from brown cardstock. Print title and journaling on vellum sheet. Layer vellum over large cardstock letter; attach black eyelets at corners. Print clip art heart design on red cardstock and crop. Attach black eyelet; dangle from antique key (personal collection) with twine.

MaryJo Regier, Memory Makers
Inspired by Tina Chambers, Sardinia, Ohio

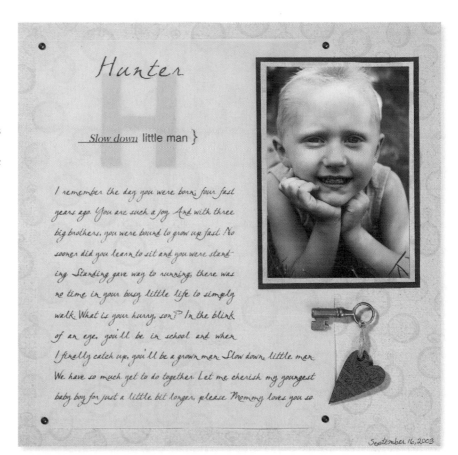

What Are You Thinking?

Hilary guesses at the thoughts that run through her son's head on a colorfully layered vellum design. Print journaling on white cardstock; trim to size. Mount computer-manipulated photo on white cardstock; layer with journaling block on black cardstock. Print title and descriptive words on yellow, pink, green, purple and blue vellums (Provo Craft). Cut words to size; layer on page as shown.

Hilary Erickson, Santa Clara, California

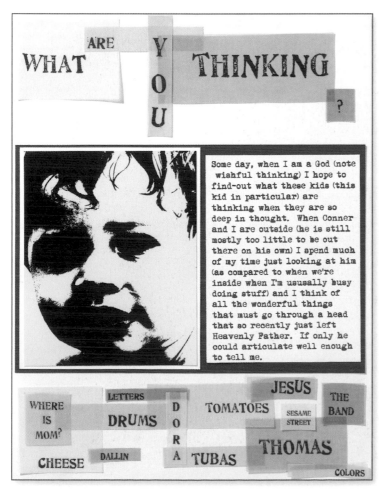

Callum John

Sometimes the simplest of activities, like climbing on a fence, can keep a busy little boy completely content. Slice a ½" strip of white cardstock and a 3½" strip of green cardstock; vertically layer at left side of brown cardstock on left page. Stamp title (Hero Arts) and leaf designs (Hero Arts) on green cardstock with brown and green inks. Tear edges around stamped leaves and attach small brad (Karen Foster Design). Cut title to size; punch a small hole at bottom of title block; dangle leaf designs from title block with fiber (On The Surface). Mount photos on white background for right page; layer printed vellum overlay (Creative Imaginations) and double-matted photo. Attach leaf design to matted photo with small brad. Complete pages with handwritten journaling.

Joanne Moseley, Aurora, Ontario, Canada

Thoughts

Valerie features her son lost in thought with expressive photos. Slice a 3¼" strip of thin corkboard (Magic Scraps); punch slots (Fiskars) along bottom edge of strip and mount 4" from top of tan cardstock. Wrap twine around page on corkboard strip and bottom of page. Mount photos on rust cardstock; tear top edge and punch slots at top of one mat. Tie twine through punched slots. Adhere sticker quote (Wordsworth) on beige cardstock; cut to size and punch slots at top. Tie twine through slots of quote and bottom of cork strip. Die cut leaves (Dayco) from brown, orange and green cardstocks; detail with chalks. Mount green and orange leaves over twine strands with self-adhesive foam spacers. Freehand cut tag from brown cardstock; collage and layer with die-cut leaves and colored torn cardstock scraps. Stamp title (Hero Arts) with green ink on brown cardstock; tear all edges and attach circle clip (Making Memories). Punch hole at top of tag and tie with fibers (Fibers By The Yard). Stamp date (Making Memories) on small white tag; attach to tag with embroidery thread. Complete page with buttons mounted on corkboard strip.

Valerie Barton, Flowood, Mississippi

Uniquely U

Michele displays her son's unique personality on a simple color-blocked page with minimal embellishment. Slice two 2½" strips of brown cardstock; horizontally mount at top and bottom of green cardstock. Layer photo matted with tan cardstock near bottom of page; mount Scrabble tile (Hasbro) at bottom right corner. Print journaling on tan cardstock; cut to size and mount next to photo. Print title on tan cardstock; silhouette cut. Tie pieces of twine into a knot; horizontally mount along top of page and on journaling block.

Michele Woods, Worthington, Ohio

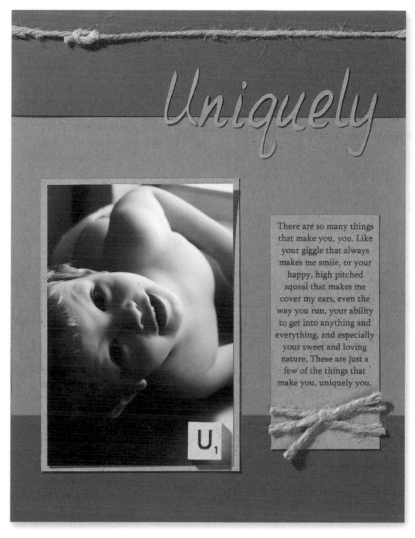

There are so many things that make you, you. Like your giggle that always makes me smile, or your happy, high pitched squeal that makes me cover my ears, even the way you run, your ability to get into anything and everything, and especially your sweet and loving nature, These are just a few of the things that make you, uniquely you.

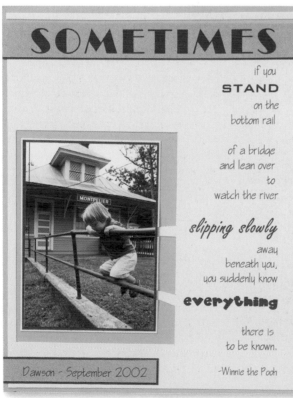

SOMETIMES

if you
STAND
on the
bottom rail

of a bridge
and lean over
to
watch the river

slipping slowly

away
beneath you,
you suddenly know

everything

there is
to be known.

-Winnie the Pooh

Dawson - September 2002

Sometimes

Like most boys, Dana's son finds it hard to resist climbing on anything within his reach. Slice a ⅛" strip of ivory cardstock; horizontally mount at top of blue cardstock. Print title, date and text on green and ivory cardstocks. Mat photo on black cardstock. Using a craft knife and ruler, slice a window with graphic design that extends horizontal lines from photo into ivory cardstock with printed journaling. Layer ivory cardstock over blue cardstock background; mount matted photo in cut-out window. Slice title and date strip; mat on black cardstock. Mount title under small ivory strip near top of page and date strip near bottom of page.

Dana Swords, Fredericksburg, Virginia

Sweet Innocence

An untended "weed patch" provides the perfect playground for Shandy's exploring toddler. Slice ½", 1" and 1¼" strips of light green cardstock and a ¼" and ½" strips of darker green cardstock. Vertically mount 1¼" and ½" light green strips and ¼" dark green strip at left side of left page over black cardstock, leaving space between slices. Horizontally mount the ½" dark green strip and 1" light green strip at top of right page. Mount photos on white cardstock; layer on page with dark green cardstock rectangle. Attach green brad fasteners (Making Memories) at corners. Print title and journaling on vellum; cut to size. Mount title at top of right page with black eyelets (Making Memories). Layer enlarged matted photo on light and dark green cardstock squares; attach black brad fasteners (Making Memories) at corners of dark green cardstock. Stamp descriptive words (Stampin' Up!) with black ink. Complete page with punched and re-punched squares (Creative Memories) randomly mounted on left page.

Shandy Vogt, Nampa, Idaho

Blessing

Kim captures a candid shot of her son in a fun and graphic layout. Tear a 3¼" strip of patterned paper (KI Memories); vertically mount on green textured cardstock. Adhere letter stickers (Creative Imaginations) on vellum silver-rimmed tag; attach tag to photo with silver eyelet. Attach silver eyelets 1¾" from top of page; string fiber through eyelets on photo and page. Adhere sentiment sticker on vellum; cut to size and attach to page with silver eyelets. Slip preprinted designs (source unknown) behind vellum pocket.

Kim Haynes, Harrah, Oklahoma

Sam, 1

Peyton

Michelle reflects her son's love of the outdoors on a page with scrapbooking rocks and torn patterned paper in warm shades of green. Double mat light green cardstock with yellow and dark green cardstocks; add pen detail around edge of light green cardstock and chalk around edge of dark green cardstock. Tear a 3" strip of patterned paper (Print Blocks). Rip strip into pieces; reassemble at left side of page to look like a mosaic, leaving space between each piece. Horizontally mount strip of netting (Magic Scraps) 1½" from top of page. Single and quadruple mat photos on white, green and yellow cardstocks. Wrap quadruple-matted photo with fibers (Magic Scraps). Freehand cut tag from white cardstock; brush with green, gray and brown chalks. Attach eyelet at top and tie with fibers. Mount torn patterned paper strip at bottom of tag with small rocks. Journal and border tag with black pen. Punch three 1¾" squares from green cardstock and two 1½" squares from patterned paper. Slice patterned paper squares on the diagonal; layer with sentiment rocks (Plaid) on green squares.

Michelle Keeth, Lowell, Arkansas

Dare

Dana captured the spirit of an adventurous little boy as he teeters on a high windowsill peering out at what is outside. Slice two 3/16" strips of patterned paper (Karen Foster Design); horizontally mount 3¾" from top of page. Cut four 2 x 2¾" rectangles from metallic paper (DMD); slice a 1½ x 2¼" window in each rectangle. Print tile and journaling on vellum; tear edges around journaling. Cut title letters to fit behind metallic paper frames. Punch small hole at top of vellum tags; string fibers (Fibers By The Yard, Rubba Dub Dub) with beads; feed through holes and wrap around top of page as shown. Hang wooden star (source unknown) and beads strung on wire from fibers. Double mat photo on orange cardstock and patterned paper; cut matting to mimic window angle as shown. Layer matted photo over vellum journaling block. Slice two ¼" strips of patterned paper; attach to page with copper eyelets (Making Memories) over journaling block.

Dana Swords, Fredericksburg, Virginia

Giggle

Elizabeth equates her son's silliness and sense of humor with a positive and confident attitude that she hopes will lead him through a happy and successful life. Double mat one photo on golden yellow and ivory cardstocks. Mat other photos on golden yellow cardstock; layer over coastal netting (Magic Scraps) at right side of page. Wrap fibers around metal word (Making Memories); mount at top of page under coastal netting. Attach concho (7 Gypsies) to penny; push prongs through page and secure at back. Tie metal letter tag (Making Memories) to coastal netting with jute string. Stain white tag (AMACO) with walnut ink; stamp letters (PSX Design) with black ink and attach with small brass brad (Lost Art Treasures) at bottom of page. Loop red waxy flax (ScrapWorks) through coastal netting and tie. Hide matted journaling on brown cardstock under focal-point photo. Stamp large flower (Impression Obsession) and word on transparency with yellow and black inks; sprinkle with embossing powder and set with a heat gun. Partially silhouette cut flower; mount on journaling mat with tiny tag and small brass brads. Stain tiny tag with walnut ink; write directive with black pen. Slide journaling under photo mat.

Elizabeth Ruuska, Rensselaer, Indiana

Pure Imagination

With a life full of scheduled play dates and activities, it's not often that a boy gets to relax and watch the clouds go by. Triple mat photo on white, red and tan cardstocks; cut mesh (Magic Mesh) photo corners and layer on matted photo. Print journaling on tan cardstock; cut to size and mat on red cardstock. Layer on page over mesh strip. Cut large title word from tan cardstock using template (Scrap Pagerz); mat on red cardstock and silhouette cut. Write first title word on tan cardstock with blue pen; cut to size and mat. Mount silver eyelet words (Making Memories) over red cardstock and mesh scrap. Adhere sticker quote (source unknown) under matted photo.

Paula DeReamer, Alexandria, Minnesota

Our Little Boy

Madeline's layout celebrates the traits her son embodies as he plays and discovers the world around him. Mount 8½ x 11" patterned paper (Provo Craft) on rust cardstock. Print title and descriptive letters in a variety of type fonts on orange cardstock; cut all to size and rub brown ink pad on edges. Cut title from green cardstock; ink around edges. Assemble title words together as shown on burlap scrap; mount red star button (Hancock Fabrics) at center of letter "O." Mat photos on orange cardstock; rub brown ink pad on edges of matting. Press brown ink pad on edges of tags (Avery); layer punched and inked feet, teddy bear, heart and hands (EK Success) on tags with descriptive words. Tie tags with fibers (source unknown) and hemp string (Darice). Attach orange star eyelets (Doodlebug Design) on largest tag. Layer plastic magnifying glass (source unknown) with descriptive word over punched dragonfly (EK Success). Stamp date (source unknown) at bottom of page with brown ink.

Madeline Fox, River Ridge, Louisiana

A Walk In The Woods

Chris photographed her son in one of his favorite settings, doing what he loves to do most on a beautiful fall day. Slice a 3⅞" strip of gold cardstock; rub brown ink pad on edges. Layer strip over torn patterned paper (C-Thru Ruler) mounted at bottom half of brown cardstock. Mount cropped photos. Attach yellow eyelets at top corners of page; string fibers (Fibers By The Yard) across page through eyelets. Assemble title from a variety of letter stickers: tag letters (EK Success), vellum letters (Mrs. Grossman's), script letters (Wordsworth) and letters mounted on brads (Creative Imaginations). Print journaling on gold cardstock; cut to size and rub ink pad on edges. Punch photos into 1¼" squares; layer on page. Crop photo into circle to fit inside vellum metal-rimmed tag (Making Memories); punch hole at top and tie with fibers. Adhere sticker words (Creative Imaginations). Complete page with thin sticks mounted with glue dots.

Chris Douglas, East Rochester, Ohio

Zachary, 2½

From the time you could walk you've loved to pick out your own clothes. Usually they are not ensembles that mommy would put together, but they are so you. Sometimes it's your yellow rubber boots paired with nothing but a diaper and a smile. Other times it's your Bob the Builder sweatshirt 3 days in a row until I sneak it away to wash it while you sleep. Yet another day you will demand Jake's spiderman t-shirt, the one that hangs down to your knees. Whatever outfit you insist on it is always utterly **LUCAS**

Lucas

Cheryl documents her son's dress code with tongue-in-cheek humor. Begin with computer-generated journaling on 8½ x 11" cardstock. Trim journaling and mount on background paper. Crop photo vertically, mount on page and embellish with metal photo corners (Making Memories).

Cheryl Overton, Kelowna, British Columbia, Canada

When I Grow Up

Cheryl preserves an "aim-high-and-reality bites" conversation with her young son through simple photos and journaling. First, print title and journaling on 8½ x 11" cardstock, using the left-justified text setting to allow room for photos down right side of page. Crop three photos. Mount one in upper right corner, another atop metal-rimmed tag (Making Memories) and the third over a strip of complementary-colored cardstock. Add tiny heart brad fastener (Provo Craft) on metal tag to finish.

Cheryl Overton, Kelowna, British Columbia, Canada

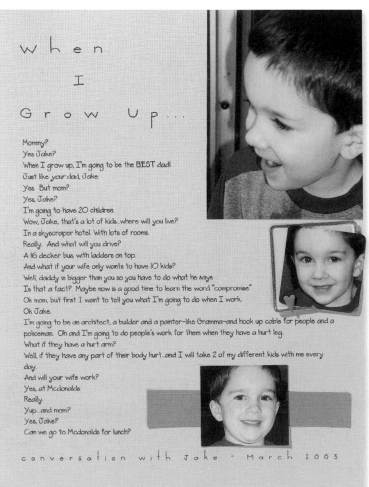

When I Grow Up...

Mommy?
Yes Jake?
When I grow up, I'm going to be the BEST dad!
Just like your dad, Jake.
Yes. But mom?
Yes, Jake?
I'm going to have 20 children.
Wow, Jake, that's a lot of kids...where will you live?
In a skyscraper hotel. With lots of rooms.
Really. And what will you drive?
A 16 decker bus, with ladders on top.
And what if your wife only wants to have 10 kids?
Well, daddy is bigger than you so you have to do what he says.
Is that a fact? Maybe now is a good time to learn the word "compromise".
Ok mom, but first I want to tell you what I'm going to do when I work.
Ok Jake.
I'm going to be an architect, a builder and a painter–like Gramma–and hook up cable for people and a policeman. Oh and I'm going to do people's work for them when they have a hurt leg.
What if they have a hurt arm?
Well, if they have any part of their body hurt...and I will take 2 of my different kids with me every day.
And will your wife work?
Yes, at Mcdonalds
Really.
Yup...and mom?
Yes, Jake?
Can we go to Mcdonalds for lunch?

conversation with Jake - March 2003

Mommy's Tulip Mistake

Instead of just looking at the first tulip of the season, Joanna's son liked its vibrant color so much that he decided to eat one! Mat one photo on red cardstock; layer with other photos on matted green cardstock. Horizontally mount netting strip (Magic Scraps) and ribbon (Offray) at bottom of page. Print title and journaling on light green paper; slice into a 2¼" strip. Mat on dark green cardstock and mount at right side of page. Crop photo to fit inside metal-rimmed tag (Making Memories); mount above title. Create flowers from layers of torn cardstock in red, green and yellow. Mount at bottom of page with paper yarn (Making Memories) to look like stems and leaves. Layer one flower with ribbon at top of page.

Joanna Bolick, Black Mountain, North Carolina

Thoughts Of Youth

Michaela captures her little boy in a rare pensive mood, looking as if he is plotting his next mischievous plan. Mount photo on white cardstock matted with rust cardstock; tear top and bottom edges. Horizontally mount on brown cardstock. Print poem on white cardstock; tear into strip and mount below photo.

Michaela Young-Mitchell, Morenci, Arizona

A Boy's Will...

Didi's son enjoys a quiet, reflective moment, leaving her wonder what is running through his mind. Slice a 3" strip of light green cardstock; horizontally mount at bottom of patterned paper (Wübie). Tear a 1½" strip of green paper and a 1" strip of patterned paper; layer atop light green cardstock. Layer photo over mulberry and light green cardstock strips before double matting on green and yellow cardstocks. Print quote and journaling on light green cardstocks; cut quote to size and tear bottom edge. Cut journaling into tag shape; double mat. Embellish with torn patterned paper strip and sticker (source unknown). Cut second tag from green cardstock; collage with stickers (Debbie Mumm), punched leaves (All Night Media, EK Success) and torn pieces of solid and patterned cardstocks. Stamp design (All Night Media) on tag with gold ink; sprinkle with gold embossing powder and set with a heat gun. Attach gold eyelets (Doodlebug Design) at top of tags; tie with fibers and layer on page.

Didi Roche, Heidelberg, Germany

Between The Innocence

The sparkling personality of Renee's son is framed with textured matting made to look like light reflecting off of an icy snow. Print title and journaling on green cardstock; mount over textured white cardstock background. Create a textured mat by painting white cardstock with modeling paste (Liquitex); while wet, sprinkle with glass beads. Let texture dry completely before using as photo mat. Triple mat photo with dark green cardstock and white textured mat; attach small silver brads (Close To My Heart) at photo corners. Attach silver snowflake charms (source unknown) with small silver brads.

Renee Foss, Seven Fields, Pennsylvania

Addison

Valerie frames a thoughtful photo of her son with a stamped list of his special qualities. Cut frame from orange cardstock; press green ink pad on frame, leaving a bit of orange showing. Sprinkle with green embossing powder; set with heat gun. Stamp leaf, postal and script writing designs (Hero Arts) with Versamark pad (Tsukineko); sprinkle with embossing powder and set with heat gun. Mat photo on orange paper; stamp words and small leaves (both Hero Arts) with green ink around photo. Mount stamped and embossed frame over matted photo. Collage background of page with a variety of patterned papers in orange and green (Paper Adventures). Layer framed photo over metal mesh on collaged background. Unwrap orange and green paper yarn (Making Memories); intertwine strands and vertically mount at right side of page. Stamp title letters (Hero Arts) with green ink; cut into circle and mount on metal-rimmed tag (Making Memories). Attach beaded chain to tag and secure around paper yarn strips. Form a rectangle from brown clay (Polyform Products); bake as directed and let cool. Press Versamark pad (Tsukineko) on rectangle; sprinkle with green speckled ultra thick embossing enamel (Stampendous). Heat from underside with an embossing gun; press leaf stamp (Hero Arts) with copper ink into enamel while still warm. Mount over paper yarn strips as shown.

Valerie Barton, Flowood, Mississippi

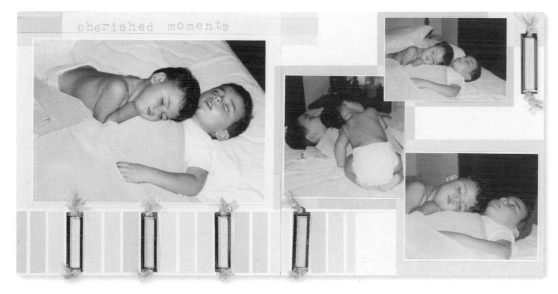

Cherished Moments

Renee's two boys share almost everything, including a peaceful nap—a stark contrast to their very active waking moments. Mat photos on white cardstock; mount on patterned background cardstock (SEI). Print title on light green cardstock; slice into ¾" strip and mount at top of page. Stamp descriptive words (PSX Design) on patterned paper; mount gold bookplates (Magic Scraps) tied with fibers (EK Success) over stamped words as shown. Carry patterned paper design on second page with cropped strips of cardstock in matching colors.

Renee Villalobos-Campa, Winnebago, Illinois

Keep The Faith

Becky writes a touching letter to her son offering love and support while he struggles through a tough transition at school. Print journaling on yellow cardstock; cut to size and layer with dark blue cardstock on black background. Slice three ¼" strips of yellow cardstock; horizontally mount at top and bottom of page as shown. Punch orange, yellow and dark blue cardstock circles to fit inside metal-rimmed tags (Avery); mount on dark blue cardstock. Adhere letter stickers (Creative Imaginations, Provo Craft) for title on orange cardstock square.

Becky Thompson, Fruitland, Idaho

Dream With Your Heart

A sweet wish is made from a mother's heart while her son sleeps soundly after a hard day at play. Re-create this computer-generated (Microsoft Picture It!) page by creating colored squares and adding texture. Add color and texture to circles. Make frame by creating a square, adding color and cropping out the center. Select the heart shape and add color to it. Finish by layering text in desired font over shapes. To create the page manually, layer enlarged and cropped photos with blue and yellow cardstock squares over textured background. Using a ruler and craft knife, slice a ¼" frame from yellow cardstock; mount atop enlarged photo, slightly askew. Punch circles in a variety of sizes for two title words from blue, yellow and tan cardstocks; stamp or adhere title letters on circles. Adhere black and white letter stickers along bottom of page to complete title; layer white stickers over red punched heart.

Rhonda Altus, Walnut Grove, Missouri

Benny Loves
His Goldfish

Sam's son is so obsessed with little goldfish crackers that he is often seen eating them in his bed and even in the bathtub. Layer photos on patterned background paper (SEI). Adhere colored circle stickers and letter stickers (Doodlebug Design) on metal-rimmed tags (Staples); attach goldfish brads on each tag. Assemble title from letter stickers (Doodlebug Design, EK Success). Print partial title and journaling on blue cardstock and transparency; cut both to size. Mount title strip with heart brads (Provo Craft). Attach fish brads above and below journaling.

Sam Cousins, Shelton, Connecticut

Obsessed? Isn't that an awfully strong word for an 18 month old boy? Not when it comes to Benny and his Goldfish crackers. In fact, there is no other word to describe Benny's love for Goldfish. We have to keep stocked up on these little snacks...heaven forbid we ever ran out. Thank goodness there is a Pepperidge Farm outlet nearby! When we go to the grocery store, he can find them on the shelf. He has learned how to get them out of the cabinet. His favorite thing to do is to pull a package out of the cabinet, climb up onto the couch, eat and watch his cartoons!!! He also loves to eat them in the car, in his bed and yes...even the bathtub!!!

Seek
The Wisdom

Margie's son gets lost in a field of thoughts and dandelions. To re-create this computer-generated layout (Adobe Photoshop 6.0), start with a black background. Enlarge photo and add a white box behind it for mat. Type quote in white text in desired fonts, highlighting a couple of the words in color to make them stand out. Add text date to complete. To make the page by hand, mount enlarged photo at center of page on white cardstock. Print quote on cardstock; slice and mount above and below photo. Color in words with yellow pen.

Margie Lundy, Greenfield, Ohio

A Cookie Or Two

Martha's son demonstrates that one is never too young to love deliciously warm chocolate chip cookies. Double mat enlarged photo on light green and blue cardstocks; mount on patterned paper (KI Memories). Mat small photo on green cardstock; layer on large laminate tag (Wilsonart) tied and wrapped with fibers (Fibers By The Yard). Print title and journaling on transparency film (Hewlett Packard); cut to size and mount above laminate tag. Embellish vellum metal-rimmed tags (Making Memories) with letter stickers (SEI), circle cropped photo and design pebble (Creative Imaginations). Tie all tags with fibers.

Martha Crowther, Salem, New Hampshire

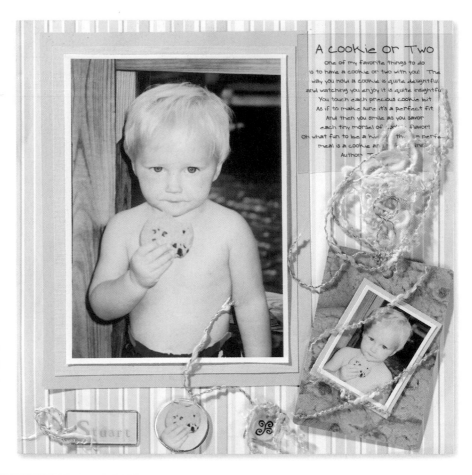

How Can I Say No?

Jlyne finds it hard to resist her son's big blue eyes that beseech "pleeeease?" Print title and journaling on peach cardstock. Mat photo on brown cardstock. Layer real candy bar wrapper and aluminum foil over preprinted die cut (Creative Imaginations) trimmed with decorative scissors.

Jlyne Hanback, Biloxi, Mississippi

Ryan, 11

Baseball Fan

Janet memorializes her son's favorite baseball shirt with soft, sepia-toned photos. Layer torn, printed paper (Wübie) with torn brown cardstock over textured burgundy cardstock. Stain brown cardstock with walnut ink (Manto Fev) for an aged look. Double mat sepia-toned photos on burgundy and navy blue cardstocks. Wrap bottom of middle photo with fibers (EK Success, Brown Bag Fibers); mount with self-adhesive foam spacers for dimension. Layer largest photo with black precut photo mat (MJ Designs) and brown corrugated cardstock (DMD) stained with walnut ink. Wrap fibers around bottom of double-matted photo; tie baseball bat button (Jesse James) with fibers. Print title and date on tags; stain with walnut ink. Mount silver nameplate (Magic Scraps) over tag; attach screw heads (Making Memories) on nameplate and tag as shown.

Janet Hopkins, Frisco, Texas

Chick

Stacy features the softer side of a rambunctious little boy and his fascination with birds. Print computer clip art (Microsoft) of chick; cut to size. Press image on Versamark pad (Tsukineko); sprinkle with clear ultra thick embossing enamel and set with a heat gun. Repeat two more times for added thickness. When cool, gently bend and crack enamel for antique look. Slice a 1¼" strip of tan cardstock; vertically mount with matted embossed images. Print journaling on tan cardstock; cut to size and mount next to enlarged photo with copper eyelets (Impress Rubber Stamps). Cut title letters from preprinted paper (source unknown).

Stacy McFadden, Doncaster East, Victoria, Australia

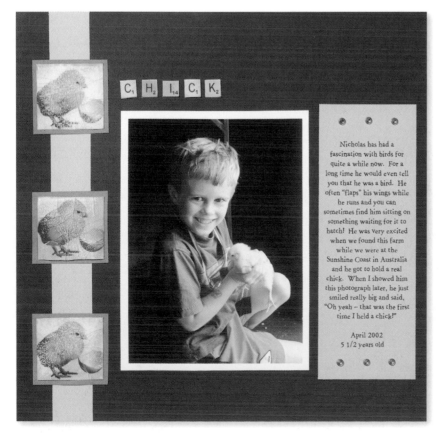

Nicholas has had a fascination with birds for quite a while now. For a long time he would even tell you that he was a bird. He often "flaps" his wings while he runs and you can sometimes find him sitting on something waiting for it to hatch! He was very excited when we found this farm while we were at the Sunshine Coast in Australia and he got to hold a real chick. When I showed him this photograph later, he just smiled really big and said, "Oh yeah – that was the first time I held a chick!"

April 2002
5 1/2 years old

It's A Boy's Life

As boys pursue their passions and childhood enthusiasms, they discover the excitement of accomplishment. Participation in individual and team sports and various other activities help boys master the craft of leadership. On the field or the court, boys learn good stress management, as well as coping and survival skills. They also learn about winning, losing and grace under fire. Born with an innate need for speed and competitiveness, boys quickly understand when it's "every man for himself" or it's "all about teamwork"—regardless of the activity. As your son manages his choices and learns from consequences, respect his play and be his biggest fan. Preserve his trials and tribulations in a scrapbook album for posterity. It's a boy's life after all!

Mitchell, 10

What lies behind us and what lies before us are tiny matters compared to what lies within us.

—Emerson

Jet!

Torrey brings the action of a fast and fierce soccer player to life with a succession of photos creatively mounted behind a light-switch plate. Layer two shades of green cardstock on dark purple cardstock for background. Die cut title, date and plane (QuicKutz) from green and purple cardstocks. Triple-mat photo on white, green and purple cardstocks. Print journaling on transparency; layer over green vellum and freehand sliced purple cardstock strips. Adhere screws on switch plate; mount succession of photos behind switch plate openings. Add dimensional details with silhouette-cut images mounted on the outside of switch plate with self-adhesive foam spacers. Mount switch plate at bottom of page. Punch and re-punch circles in graduating sizes from green and purple cardstocks; randomly mount on page as shown.

Torrey Miller, Thornton, Colorado

A Formula For Fun...

Boys and dirt just seem to go together, and there's no better way for a boy to get his fill thrills and dust than by driving off-road vehicles! Print title and journaling on tan cardstock; slice into 2¼" strips; mount ½" from top and bottom of black cardstock. Slice a second 2¼" strip of tan cardstock, and two ¼" and two ½" strips of blue cardstock. Horizontally mount tan and blue strips on pages as shown, carrying design onto both pages; attach screw eyelets (Making Memories) at ends of blue strips. Slice two ¼" strips of red cardstock; layer red strip over enlarged sliced photo mounted on both pages. Crop four photos into 2⅛" squares; mount metal frame (Making Memories) atop one photo. Mat another photo on red cardstock; attach silver frame corner (Making Memories). Complete page with letter eyelets (Making Memories) attached to journaling block.

Diana Hudson, Bakersfield, California
Photos: Mona Shield Payne, Henderson, Nevada

Jake, 6

Diggin' Dirt

Lisa's boys demonstrate their love of getting down and dirty with rough and ready off-road bikes in the desert. Tear strips of vellum and patterned paper (Karen Foster Design); crumple and flatten one vellum strip. Horizontally and vertically mount torn strips on both beige pages as shown. Adhere title sticker (Karen Foster Design) on vellum. Triple mat photo on left page with black and yellow cardstocks and green mulberry paper; tear top edge of first mat and all edges of mulberry paper. Mat photos on right page with black and yellow cardstocks and mulberry paper. Layer small photos over torn patterned paper at bottom of right page; layer large photo on red corrugated cardstock with torn edges. Stitch vellum to page with red hemp string as shown. Complete page with journaling using green and red pens.

Lisa Brown, Maricopa, Arizona

Live It Boy Style

Boys of any age need only a ball and an open field to be free, wild and reckless. Mat gray cardstock squares and rectangles with black cardstock. Mount on patterned paper (Faux Memories) background. Mat large photo on black cardstock; layer photos over matted blocks. Print journaling on gray cardstock; cut to size and mat on black cardstock. Adhere title and quote stickers (Creative Imaginations) on white cardstock; cut to size and attach to page with small black brads (Hyglo/American Pin). Stamp date (Staples) at bottom of right page.

Maryann Wise, Bakersfield, California

Give Me A Place To Stand

MaryJo's sophisticated sports layout reflects the serious game her 11-year-old now plays, where the score really counts and the players implement strategic offensive and defensive plays. Layer photocopied offensive and defensive team plays under vellum; mount at bottom half of golden cardstock. Print title and journaling on white cardstock; layer at top half of page with ¼" green cardstock slice. Crop photos into 1⅞" strips; mount under title. Adhere sticker tags (EK Success); write title and player number with green pen using template (The Crafter's Workshop). Stamp football image (Provo Craft) on one tag; sprinkle with copper embossing powder and set with a heat gun. Apply brown ink to bottom of football cleat; press onto vellum at bottom of page for a unique and realistic embellishment.

MaryJo Regier, Memory Makers

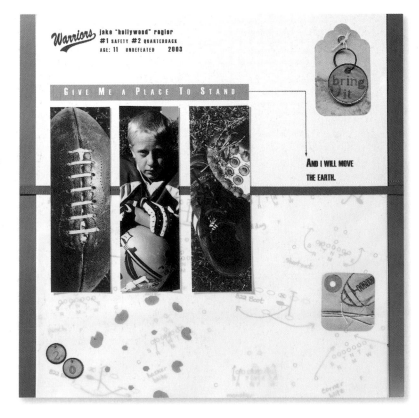

O Running Stream

Nancy captures her son in midflight demonstrating his skillful in-line skating talent and technique. Slice a 2" strip of blue sparkle cardstock (source unknown); vertically mount on gray cardstock. Layer photos. Print quote on vellum; slice into a strip. Attach to page with silver eyelets (Making Memories).

Nancy McCoy, Gulfport, Mississippi

O Running Stream Of Sparkling Joy,
To Be A Soaring Human Boy
Charles Dickens

Reid

Nanette's little boy transforms from an average 5-year-old to a determined and focused athlete as soon as he hits the ice. Single and double mat photos on blue, red and yellow cardstocks. Print journaling on vellum; cut to size and detail with pen and chalks. Mount photos on patterned background paper (Scrappin' Sports and More) matted on blue cardstock. Layer vellum over photos; secure with blue and red eyelets. Attach metal word eyelets (Making Memories) on vellum to complete journaling. Cut letters for title from preprinted paper (Hot Off The Press); layer on matte metal scraps (source unknown). Cut into circles and fold in around edges; pierce hole and tie fiber. Hang letters from fibers mounted with small silver brads (Making Memories) across bottom of page.

Nanette Witt, Addison, Illinois

Brett

A small baseball fan stands on the sidelines, waiting and dreaming about when it will be his turn to take the field. Layer preprinted frame (Leeco) over cropped photo. Adhere quote sticker (Wordsworth) on ivory cardstock; cut to size and mount with square eyelets (Chatterbox). Mount baseball image tags (Leeco) on page. Stamp title and date (PSX Design) on vellum; cut to size and attach to tags with silver eyelets (Happy Hammer).

Amy Madzinski, Naperville, Illinois

Robert Liberatore

Martha accompanies a casual portrait with a young man's list of favorite activities. Double mat photo on blue cardstock and patterned paper (KI Memories); layer on blue cardstock. Cut gray patterned paper (KI Memories) into tag shape; mat on patterned paper. Punch hole at top, tie with fibers (Fibers By The Yard) and drape one fiber strand zigzig down the front of tag. Print title and text on transparency; cut to size and mount above and on tag. Mount mosaic tiles (Magic Scraps) alternated with letter beads (Wal-Mart) below matted photo.

Martha Crowther, Salem, New Hampshire

Baseball

Christina documents the progress of a young athlete whose love for the game and confidence intensified after a successful season. Slice a 3¾" strip of taupe cardstock and two 3" strips of baseball image photo art (Microsoft Picture It). Mount taupe cardstock at top of left page. Vertically mount baseball images at bottom of left page and top of right page as shown. Layer tan cardstock with torn edge over photo image on left page. Brush torn cardstock with brown chalk. Tear a 4¾" strip of tan cardstock and a 1" strip of black cardstock; layer at bottom of right page. Print title and journaling on transparency; cut to size and layer on tan cardstock. Attach silver baseball charm (source unknown) on spiral clip (Target); clip to matted photo. Mount cropped photo behind metal frame (Making Memories); layer with enlarged photo on left page.

Christina Chrushch, Rocky Mount, North Carolina

Kameron, 6

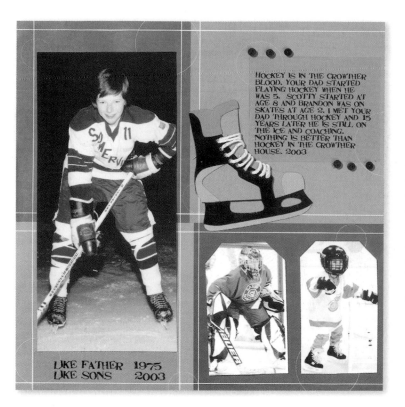

Like Father, Like Sons

Martha documents a father's love of hockey which is passed down to his sons. Cut two photos into tag shapes; mount all photos on patterned paper (Colorbōk) background. Print title and journaling on transparency; cut to size. Mount small buttons (Jesse James) above and below journaling block. Paper piece skate from black, gray and brown cardstocks; punch holes and lace with string.

Martha Crowther, Salem, New Hampshire

Countdown To Hockey

An eagerly anticipated hockey season has Linda's son trying on his gear six months in advance. Horizontally mount blue ribbon (Offray) across bottom of page; layer with hockey stickers (source unknown) adhered on white matted squares. Double mat photos on red and black cardstocks. Create a lift-up photo mat with hidden journaling: cut a 3¾ x 10" piece of black cardstock; using a ruler and bone folder, score at 5" and fold over. Print journaling on vellum; mat and mount under flap with clear photo corners. Punch stars (EK Success) from red cardstock; mount on page with small gold brads (Creative Impressions). Print title on vellum; cut to size and mount at top of page with clear photo corners.

Linda Abrams, Thornhill, Ontario, Canada

All Star Basketball

A love for the game can start early in a boy's life as Cindy discovers with her 2½-year-old son. Crop patterned paper (Mustard Moon) into a large square and rectangle; mat on blue cardstock and layer with cropped photos. Cut title from blue paper using template (Chatterbox); layer two letters on silver-rimmed tags (American Tag Co.) before mounting on brown cardstock. Attach orange eyelets (Impress Rubber Stamps); loop string through eyelets under photo on left page. Adhere basketball sticker (Provo Craft) on brown cardstock; silhouette cut and layer on silver-rimmed tag as shown.

Cindy Harris, Modesto, California

Sweet Victory

Denise features her son's basketball medal on a layout that pays tribute to a winning season. Double mat enlarged photo with textured (Freckle Press) and black cardstocks. Freehand draw basketball lines on textured cardstock; using a craft knife, slice along drawn lines. Reassemble on black cardstock, leaving space between pieces; use as a photo mat. Print title and journaling on transparency; emboss with clear powder and set with heat gun. Cut title block to size and layer on cropped patterned paper (Hot Off The Press). Scan medal and print two copies; silhouette cut. Mount one atop the other with self-adhesive foam spacers. Mat small photo on black cardstock; mount with self-adhesive foam spacers over journaling and patterned paper. Print journaling on vellum, trim to fit metal tag (Making Memories) and adhere.

Denise Tucker, Versailles, Indiana

L ife's battles don't always go to the stronger or faster man.

But sooner or later

the man who wins,

is the man who

thinks he can.

Vince Lombardi

The harder you
work,
the harder
it is to
surrender.
Colt Regier
#63
Nose Tackle
Dakota Ridge
Eagles   2001

Life's Battles

As a young athlete matures, he (hopefully!) realizes there's more to learn in sports than simply playing the game. Print title quote and player information on white cardstock; slice into a 5¼" strip and mount on navy blue textured cardstock. Mat large photo on brown textured cardstock and small photos behind large slide mounts (Design Originals). Attach rivets (Chatterbox) at bottom of slide mounts; mount slides on page with self-adhesive foams spacers. Crop brown textured cardstock (Freckle Press) into square and rectangle; pierce holes and weave string through holes to resemble football lacing.

MaryJo Regier, Memory Makers

Ryan, 11

Spring 2003

Chris highlights her son on the playing field doing what he loves to do, playing soccer! Slice a 5½" strip of black cardstock and a 3½" strip of red cardstock; vertically and horizontally mount at left side of page over white cardstock for a color-blocked background. Print journaling on vellum; cut to size and mount over black cardstock strip with small black brads (Hyglo/American Pin). Mat large photo on black cardstock; layer with cropped photos and horizontally mounted black and white strips.

Chris Douglas, East Rochester, Ohio

Soccer Club

Renae's simple layout reflects the maturity her son is gaining through playing soccer. Triple mat photo with red, black and gray cardstocks. Print journaling on white speckled cardstock; mat and layer with mesh strip (Magic Mesh) over matted gray cardstock. Attach buttons (Jesse James) at right of journaling block with wire. Mount silver letters (Making Memories) and star mesh eyelets (Making Memories) above and below journaling block. Assemble title from silver tag letters (Making Memories), swirl clip (Target), letter stickers (Creative Imaginations) and pre-printed letters (DMD). Adhere letter stickers on corrugated red cardstock scrap and vellum silver-rimmed tag (Making Memories). Layer assembled title on mesh strip and matted gray cardstock. Attach star button with wire; mount alphabet beads. Layer matted photo, title and journaling blocks on patterned paper (Bo Bunny Press) matted on red paper. Complete page with silver mesh stars attached at each corner.

Renae Clark, Mazomanie, Wisconsin

Oh Boy

A boy learns by doing...even if that means not doing it right, as Colin realized when puttering with the brakes on his bicycle. Double mat large photo on black and white cardstocks; ink edges of white mat with black ink pad and mount screw eyelets (Making Memories) at corners. Mat tan cardstock background. Mount two photos at right side of page. Print journaling on white cardstock; trim to size and ink edges with black ink pad. Mount screw eyelets at top of journaling block. Adhere title sticker (Creative Imaginations) at left side of page.

Chris Douglas, East Rochester, Ohio

My Brother's Bike

Cheryl captures her son's coveting of his brother's bike with simplistic, playful colors and insightful words. Double mat photos and arrange loosely on cardstock background page to help determine placement of journaling. Computer-print journaling on cardstock background. Mount matted photos in place to complete.

Cheryl Overton, Kelowna, British Columbia, Canada

Boys Will Be Boys!

Tracy preserves her boys' sharing of a dirt bike and fondness of mud with a "mud-splattered" background. Push an old, clean toothbrush onto an ink pad. Splatter ink across background pages by running your thumbnail across the brush bristles facedown over paper. Add cropped and matted photos, title and journaling to complete.

Tracy Young, Jordanville, New York

Ready To Roll

A pack of boys take off for the neighborhood bike park ready to challenge one another and brave the steep ramps. Freehand cut a bike ramp from purple cardstock. Cut tire from black cardstock using decorative scissors. Paper piece forks and balance of bike rim from gray and red cardstocks; mount spiral clip (Target) at center of wheel. Mat photos on colored cardstocks; layer on paper-pieced background. Complete page with written title and journaling on bike ramp.

Ruthann Grabowski, Yorktown, Virginia

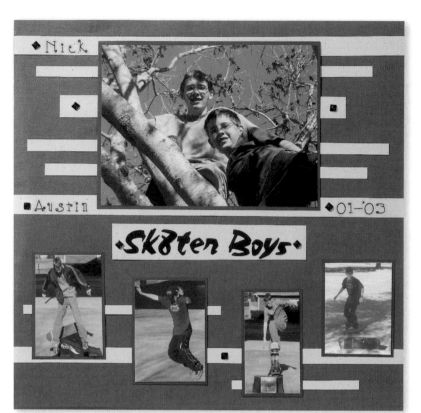

Sk8ter Boys

Ronna's sons show off their skateboarding skills and prove that two brothers can enjoy the same activity or just hanging out together. Slice ten strips of tan cardstock in varying widths. Randomly mount on gray cardstock background as shown. Mat all photos on blue cardstock; layer photos on tan strips. Adhere title and journaling letter stickers (Creative Imaginations, Provo Craft). Attach black square eyelets (Making Memories) on a few tan strips.

Ronna Waller, Houston, Texas

Bulls Eye!

Susan's son found that practice makes perfect, especially when it comes to the challenging sport of archery. Add texture to ivory and green cardstocks by dampening, crumpling and then flattening. When dry, single and double mat photos on textured cardstocks. Tear two 4½" strips of patterned paper (Cut-It-Up); horizontally mount on blue cardstock stamped with fleur-de-lis design (Close To My Heart) and Versamark ink (Tsukineko). Print title letters and journaling on red cardstock and vellum; silhouette title letters and mount at top of page. Cut journaling to size; tear bottom edge before mounting over patterned paper. Attach small silver brads and fiber at top corners of journaling block. Freehand cut ovals from red cardstock; mount at right of page to look like target. Freehand craft arrow from yellow toothpick, fibers (Fibers By The Yard) and black cardstock arrow point. Horizontally mount fibers along bottom of page; secure with small silver brads.

Susan Stringfellow, Cypress, Texas

Bowling

Gemiel documents a developmental milestone when her son's bowling technique changed from a simple push down the lane to an actual throw. Horizontally and vertically mount 1½" strips of mesh (Magic Mesh) on left and right pages. Cut title from patterned paper (NRN Designs) using template (Scrap Pagerz); mat on red cardstock and silhouette cut before mounting on mesh strip. Single and double mat photos on white, black and red cardstocks; mount mosaic tiles on second mat of one double-matted photo. Embellish tags (DMD) with red eyelets (Prym Dritz), fibers (Fibers By The Yard), bowling stickers (Frances Meyer) and mosaic tiles (Magic Scraps). Mat largest tag on black cardstock; silhouette cut and write journaling with black pen. Mount word tiles (source unknown) at top of right page on mesh strip.

Gemiel Matthews, Yorktown, Virginia

Kody, 10

He Who Has The Most Tackle Wins

Nothing keeps a group of boys busier than a body of water, a few fishing poles and a box full of tackle. Print title and names on blue vellum and blue background paper (Design Originals). Cut a 6" piece of tan paper; tear top and bottom edges and layer on blue paper. Mount photos at bottom of page to give the illusion of a single panoramic photo. Cut vellum title block to size; mount on tan cardstock with stamped hand and fish (Postmodern Design) images. Mount metal letter charms (Making Memories) on vellum to complete title. Freehand cut stamped cardstock into tag; mat on blue paper and silhouette cut. Tie with fibers (source unknown) and wrap with fishing line. Mount fishing lures at end of tag and above photo as shown. Adhere fishing equipment rub-ons (ChartPak); add shine with crystal lacquer (Sakura Hobby Craft).

MaryJo Regier, Memory Makers

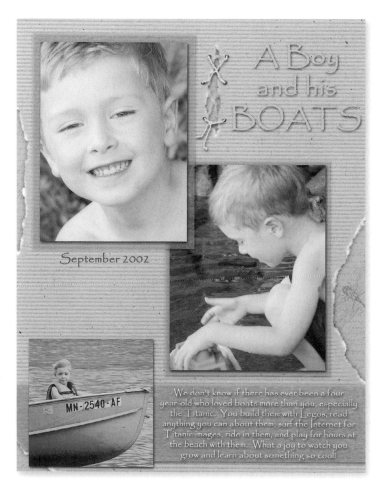

A Boy And His Boats

Michelle documents her little boy's love of boats on a page created on the computer (Adobe Photoshop Elements). Start by scanning a piece of torn, corrugated cardboard. Layer over tinted, clip art background to mimic stamping. Use the pen or pencil tool to make two-tone scratch marks to mimic fibers; add a shadow for depth. Layer title, journaling and "matted" photos, adding shadows for depth. To make the page by hand, begin with corrugated cardstock, vellum and patterned paper. Tear one hole and a few edges from brown corrugated cardstock; layer over green patterned paper. Attach eyelets on sides of tear; lace and tie with green fibers. Mat two photos on green vellum; layer on page. Print journaling on green vellum; slice into a 2½" strip. Rip away bottom left corner and mount at bottom of page. Print title on transparency and mount on page or adhere letter stickers for title.

Michelle Shefveland, Sauk Rapids, Minnesota

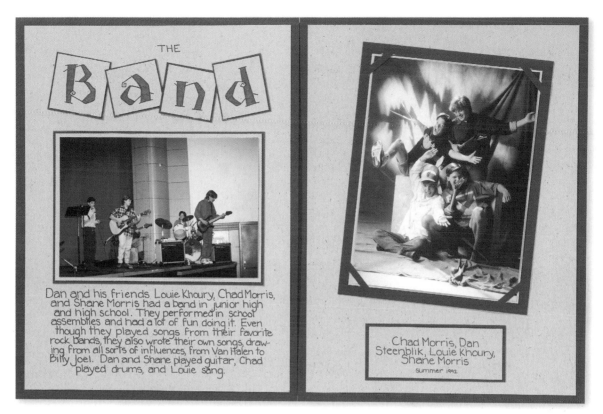

The Band

Every rock band has to start somewhere and Heidi's boys made their debut at a junior high school. Double mat photos on tan and green cardstocks. Punch corners on second mat of one photo with corner slot punch (Family Treasures). Freehand write title letters on tan cardstock squares with black and green pens; mat on green cardstock and layer at top of left page. Write balance of title and journaling with black pen.

Heidi Dillon, Salt Lake City, Utah

It's Just A Game

Susan's son proudly played the trombone in his high school band, enjoying the high-energy performances at football game half-times. Mount black patterned cardstock (Club Scrap) over yellow cardstock; draw borderlines around yellow cardstock with black pen. Cut some title letters from black cardstock using a template (Scrap Pagerz); adhere sticker letters (EK Success) to complete title. Mount photo on yellow cardstock; cut photo corners from black vellum. Adhere gold letter stickers (Provo Craft) on black cardstock square matted with yellow cardstock. Mount trombone die cut (Stamping Station) and musical note stickers (Mrs. Grossman's).

Sue Kelemen, St. Louis, Missouri

Western Things
and
Chicken Wings

Ryan has always loved music. Even before he
was born, music would calm him and as
a baby, interest him for great lengths of
time. As a toddler, I was amazed at how well
he could sing, remembering both words and
tunes of songs he'd heard only once or twice.

At the age of 5, Ryan started wanting to play the
guitar like his older cousin Matthew was learning
to. Since Matthew was saving up for his own
electric guitar, Aunt Josie let Ryan
have her old acoustic one.

Oh how he loves that old guitar! He doesn't know how
to play a single chord, but he pretends he
does, and makes up countless songs on that old
thing. One day I heard him singing with a
country twang. I couldn't make out all the
words, but I kept hearing "...Western things and
chicken wings..." as the chorus. I laughed my
head off as I asked him where he'd heard that
song. He insisted that he had made it up all
by himself. I'm pretty sure he did, as I've
heard no country musician singing about
"Western things and chicken wings!" Leave
it to Ryan to make up something as silly and
original as that! I can't wait to hear what
he comes up with next!

Western Things
And Chicken Wings

Linda details her son's talent and love of music for creating songs without ever
having a lesson. Slice a 5¼" piece of patterned paper (Magenta); mount over rust
cardstock. Randomly stamp musical notes (Rubber Stampede) with Versamark
ink (Tsukineko) on page; sprinkle with embossing powder and set with heat gun.
Print title and journaling on tan cardstock; cut to size and brush brown chalk
around edges. Mat title block on brown cardstock; layer journaling blocks with
1½" strips of brown cardstock over green and rust cardstocks. Attach star brad
fasteners (HyGlo/American Pin) at top and bottom of each brown strip. Single
and triple mat photos on rust, olive green and tan cardstocks. Attach eyelets near
top of second mat on triple-matted photo; tie hemp string through eyelets across
top of photo as shown. Attach eyelets (Making Memories) at the bottom corners
of one photo and the top corners of another; tie together with hemp string. Layer
tied photos over 2¼" tan cardstock strip with ¼" green cardstock strips mounted
at top and bottom. Attach star brads between photos. Layer matted photos on
right page with patterned paper; attach eyelets and tie together with hemp string.

Linda Rodriguez, Corpus Christi, Texas

Ryan, 11

A Beautiful Mind

Ruthann nurtures her son's creative mind, giving him opportunity and encouragement to draw and paint. Begin with patterned paper background (Print Blocks). Mount reduced copies of artwork, patterned paper (Creative Imaginations) and photos behind tags (DMD); tie with fibers (Ties That Bind). Mat title block and artwork on rust cardstock. Write title and journaling with black pen; mount fibers around title. Adhere sticker quote (Wordsworth) at the left side of page.

Ruthann Grabowski, Yorktown, Virginia

Let's Create Some Fun!

Three busy boys keep their hands occupied and minds active creating colorful PlayDoh designs. Slice ¼" strips of red, green, purple, blue and yellow cardstocks. Mount around edges of white cardstock background. Using a ruler and craft knife, slice a ¼" frame from white cardstock; mount over colored strips. Roll colored clay (Polyform Products) into thin strips; shape into letters and bake as directed. Mount at top of page as part of title. Adhere letter stickers (Creative Imaginations) to complete title. Mat large photos on colored cardstocks; crop other photos into squares. Print journaling on vellum; cut to size and mount over clay cut with plastic cookie cutter. Punch colored cardstock into 1" squares; mount at page corners.

Kelly Angard, Highlands Ranch, Colorado

Touch Heaven Little Men

Torrey documents the woeful tale of two brothers who lose a treasured remote-controlled airplane. Horizontally and vertically mount aluminum sheeting strips (AMACO); attach to page with small silver brads (Making Memories). Single and double mat photos on white and red cardstocks. Print journaling, descriptive words and photo captions on transparency; cut to size and mount atop aluminum sheeting, photo, photo mat and red cardstock. Attach silver brads at corners of large double-matted photo and journaled transparencies layered over red cardstock. Firmly press black ink pad (Tsukineko) on silver word dog tags; lightly wipe ink off letters, leaving a bit of shading around each word. Mount dog tags (Chronicle Books) on page with silver brads. Complete page by vertically mounting silver bead chain on right page.

Torrey Miller, Thornton, Colorado

A True Warrior

Nicholas transforms himself from a sweet and playful little boy into a fierce warrior the minute he steps into a karate studio. Print journaling on blue paper; slice into a 5⅛" piece and vertically mount at center of navy blue cardstock. Slice orange and blue solid and patterned papers into a variety of widths; vertically mount on navy blue cardstock as shown. Mat photos on orange and blue cardstocks; layer and mount one photo with self-adhesive foam spacers for dimension. Machine stitch rows ¼" apart on 1¼" orange paper strips to resemble a karate belt. Crisscross strips on page and mount. Adhere layered letter stickers (Creative Imaginations, Making Memories) on "belt." Freehand cut and layer yin-yang symbol from black and white cardstocks.

Kelly Angard, Highlands Ranch, Colorado

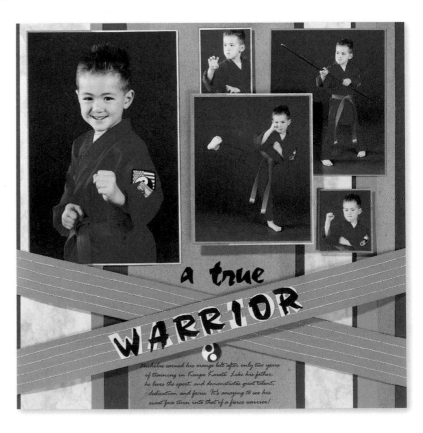

Troop 730

Taylor takes his scouting responsibilities and achievements quite seriously, working diligently toward the goal of becoming an Eagle Scout. Tear window from brown cardstock; mount over large piece of blue cardstock and tear a smaller window. Gently roll edges of brown and blue cardstocks. Mount photo behind torn windows on navy blue cardstock. Attach square brads and hemp string around torn windows. Slice a 4½" piece of patterned paper (Autumn Leaves) and a 6" piece of red patterned paper (Provo Craft); tear one edge of each and layer at left side of page. Single and double mat three photos on red patterned paper and blue and gold cardstocks. Mount single matted photo at bottom of page; attach gold eyelets at corners. Loop hemp string through eyelets; knot and tie to hemp string frame around top photo. Mount small matted photo on large piece of red cardstock; tear window at bottom of cardstock. Roll edges back in similar fashion to large torn windows. Print journaling on vellum; layer over patterned paper behind torn window. Mat on blue cardstock. Adhere title sticker letters (Frances Meyer) on blue cardstock; cut to size and triple mat. Re-create troop number patches by adhering number stickers (Creative Memories) on red cardstock; double mat on red patterned paper and white cardstock. Attach brads and tied hemp string above and below troop number as shown. Complete page by adhering number and letter stickers on page for name and date.

Kelly Angard, Highlands Ranch, Colorado

Boys Will Be Boys

Boys are nothing less than strength, boldness and a sense of adventure. Bursts of physical energy tangle vigorously with risk-taking and wild abandon. Boys also possess a sense of mastery with, and intrigue for, almost anything that girls find repulsive. From fireflies, frogs and turtles, to sea-monster masks, worm hunting and muddy escapades, boys are born to reclaim their connection with nature. They also like to test themselves through a wide range of challenges, which could be why boys like to fix, build or otherwise disman-tle almost anything around them. Enter his world carefully and docu-ment it diligently. Embrace your son's boyhood with warm humor and plenty of armor, for it's a wild ride on the male side of town!

Kameron, 6

Kody, 10

Boys want to know three simple things: Who's the boss? What are the rules? And are you going to enforce 'em?

–Lew Powers, Veteran Boy Scout

Froggie

Martha features the catch of the day when her little boys ventured out to hunt for bugs. Mount patterned vellum (Chatterbox) at top of patterned paper (Chatterbox). Mat large photo with blue cardstock; mount on patterned vellum. Horizontally mount fibers (Fibers By The Yard) across bottom of matted photo. Mat three photos on blue cardstock; mount at bottom of page. Mount die-cut ladybugs and bug collector (Li'l Davis Designs).

Martha Crowther, Salem, New Hampshire

You Gotta Look Cool

A fun goggled mask can make the kindest of boys feel like mean water monsters and, of course, are very cool accessories for the pool. Print title and journaling on transparency; cut to size and layer with photos on patterned paper (NRN Designs). Tie plastic star (source unknown) with fibers (Fibers By The Yard); mount at bottom of journaling block.

Martha Crowther, Salem, New Hampshire

Kameron, 6

That Boyhood Glow

The glowing personality of a young boy shines, lighting up the world around him. Turn off the lights to watch the page glow. Mat green patterned paper (Pebbles) with blue and black cardstocks. Machine stitch zigzag pattern around edge of green patterned paper using glow-in-the-dark thread (Y.L.I.). To create fireflies, punch jumbo stars (Family Treasures) from brown cardstock; re-punch star tips with egg punch (EK Success) to shape wings. Oval punch (Punch Bunch) body from fluorescent yellow cardstock. Glue yellow body to backside of wings. Punch small circle from brown cardstock; layer at one end of body. Punch small circle in yellow body with hole punch. Randomly punch holes in matted cardstock background using an "anywhere" punch (Making Memories) making space for lights. Push small light bulbs (Crafts Etc.) through background paper; secure with "o" rings on front of page. Place crafted fireflies over lights, using small foam spacers to "lift" fireflies off page. Stamp jar image with black ink on transparency; emboss with clear embossing powder and set with heat gun. Slice thin strips of green cardstock; layer as blades of grass behind "jars" with fireflies; mount transparent "jars" over lights with glue dots. Print title letters and journaling on transparency; emboss with clear embossing powder and cut to size. Cut large title letters from fluorescent yellow cardstock using template (EK Success); paint with glow-in-the-dark paint (Duncan). Roll out glow-in-the-dark Sculpey clay (Polyform Products) into desired thickness; shape into rectangle and press into letter shapes with clay cutters (Provo Craft). Bake as directed. Layer transparent journaling block on cool clay; mount on blue cardstock. Double mat large photo with white and black cardstocks; machine stitch around photo on first mat with glow-in-the-dark thread. Crop smaller photos; layer over fluorescent yellow strip at bottom of page with clay letters. Draw firefly trails with black pen; trace over with glow-in-the-dark paint. Mount entire page onto foam core with cut-out in back to house battery pack for lights.

Torrey Miller, Thornton, Colorado

Adventure Is Worthwhile

Boys seem to be attracted to mud and water, especially if it's a big puddle of muddy water. To make this computer-generated page (Scrapbook Factory Deluxe), Rhonda scanned embossed paper and tinted the color to match the red plaid paper. Mimic the look of vellum tags in photo-editing software (Mircrosoft Picture It!) by making rings; add a metallic illusion to the rings. Mimic vellum by fading white circles. Complete with journaling in desired fonts. To achieve this look by hand, start with textured and patterned paper sliced into strips in a variety of widths; mount on white cardstock background, leaving space between strips. Mat photos on black cardstock. Adhere black letter stickers on vellum metal-rimmed tags; attach to page with jump rings. Print title on vellum; cut to size and mount below large photo.

Rhonda Altus, Walnut Grove, Missouri

Just Dump It!

Rhonda's son comes up with a philosophy to live by after spending a long time struggling with a water bucket. Re-create this computer-generated (Microsoft Picture It!) layout by starting with a tan background and add texture to it. For yellow striped background, add yellow lines to a white background. For striped background, add multicolored stripes to a white background. For patterned background, draw various shapes on a green background and use the embossing technique to add dimension. Create buttons and fibers with circles, lines and dots; color as needed to complement photo. Scan in leather knot, crop around it and layer onto layout. Fade a white square to mimic vellum and type journaling over it. To create the look of this page by hand, layer a variety of patterned papers for the background. Mat photos on black cardstock. Print title and journaling on patterned paper and vellum. Cut to size and layer with photos. Mount green and yellow buttons and knotted leather strands on page as shown.

Rhonda Altus, Walnut Grove, Missouri

Don't Go Through Life...

Rhonda frames photos of her son engaged in an average day of play. Re-create this computer-generated page (Scrapbook Factory Deluxe) by first scanning a piece of burlap for background and layering on a maroon background. Create the clock using circular shapes and Roman numerals. Create the chain by duplicating several times over a small circular gray circle. For the tag, use photo-editing software (Microsoft Picture It!) and make a ring shape appear metallic with the illusion technique. Mimic vellum by fading a white circle. Create game piece letters by adding a tan background to a san serif fonts. Type title over background in desired font. Scan actual frames (Making Memories) to use as placeholder in digital layout, then place actual frames over images when computer layout is complete. To make page by hand, create a tag with rust cardstock layered over patterned paper. Stamp clock design on ivory cardstock; silhouette cut and mount at top and bottom of page. Slice four photos into 1" strips; mount on vellum strip. Attach eyelets at end of vellum. Print title on transparency; cut to size and mount on page. Crop photos to fit behind metal frames. Write date on vellum metal-rimmed tag; attach eyelet and hang with fiber from black brad attached to page. Vertically mount Scrabble tiles at bottom of page.

Rhonda Altus, Walnut Grove, Missouri

It's A Spring Thing

Renae captures a couple of fearless "ninjas" in the midst of a fierce battle, armed with stick "swords." Tear two strips from rust cardstock; mount remaining three pieces on gray background paper (Chatterbox), leaving space between ripped pieces. Mat photos on taupe and green cardstocks; tear the bottom edge of green matting. Print title, journaling and date on green and gray cardstocks and vellum. Paper tear around title words on green cardstock; layer with large title word silhouette cut using decorative scissors. Cut journaling block to size; tear top and bottom edges. Pierce holes at two left corners; stitch with fibers (EK Success) and mount leaf buttons. Mount date at bottom of page on gray cardstock with leaf buttons (Jesse James). Freehand cut tags from gray cardstock; embellish with matted photo squares, torn cardstock strips, leaf and metal word eyelets (Making Memories). Pierce holes at top right corner and lower left corner of background over torn strips with paper piercing tool; stitch with fibers.

Renae Clark, Mazomanie, Wisconsin

Slip Slidin' Away

Leave it to three fun-lovin' boys to turn a few large pieces of cardboard into a driveway slide. Single mat photos on gray and rust cardstocks. Slice two ½" strips of blue, rust and yellow cardstocks; horizontally and vertically mount on gray cardstock square. Layer matted photo on torn brown corrugated cardstock (DMD); mount over colored strips as shown. Mat succession of three photos on light gray cardstock. Print title, journaling and names on vellum. Cut title and journaling to size; tear top and bottom edges. Horizontally mount along matted photos at bottom of page. Mount all pieces on blue cardstock background.

Danielle Donaldson, Granite Bay, California

Guys

Boredom can drive a bunch of boys to come up with some crazy ideas, including offering up themselves for sale! Mat photo on patterned paper (Scrap Ease); tear edges and brush with green chalk. Layer with green torn patterned paper strip (Scrap Ease) vertically mounted on patterned paper background (EK Success). Write journaling on tan cardstock; pierce holes and stitch with jute string. Mat on green patterned paper; tear edges and brush with brown chalk. Attach large eyelets (Creative Imaginations); loop with jute string and hang from black brad attached to page. Write date on tan cardstock; crop into tag shape using template (Deluxe Designs). Tie with jute string and mount over torn paper strip. Rip away section of cardboard; write title with black pen.

Kelly Lautenbach, Omaha, Nebraska

A Boy Is A Joy

One of Bonnie's favorite characteristics embodied by her son is his ability to seek out the great adventures in life. Mat patterned paper (EK Success) on red cardstock for background. Single and triple mat photos on brown and red cardstocks; tear edges of brown matting. Print journaling, quote and date on tan cardstock; cut to size and tear edges of journaling blocks. Brush edges with brown chalk. Cut out preprinted title and accents (EK Success); layer on torn brown paper squares, mesh (Magic Mesh) and red cardstock. Pierce holes in photo corners; feed hemp string (Westrim) through faux eyelets. Enhance accents and journaling blocks with knotted hemp string. Use page layout template (Deluxe Designs) for placement of all pieces.

Bonnie Frank, Willow Springs, Illinois

Mitchell, 10

All Boy

Vonda showcases two of
the things that make her
little boy special...his exuberant energy and zest for life. Mat photos on blue cardstock; mount
one photo over tan cardstock corners bordered with black pen. Assemble title and treasures in
pockets with paper-piecing pattern (Bumper Crops) from green, blue, brown, yellow and rust
cardstocks. Embellish pockets with buttons and stitching with embroidery floss (DMC); mount
bubble eyes on frog. Write quote and name/date on tan cardstock with black pen; detail around
edges with pen and brown chalk. Mount stitched buttons on quote block. Mount rust photo
corners on outside corners of both pages; detail with black pen.

Vonda Kirkpatrick, Wenatchee, Washington

Park

A day at the park lets a child's imagination and sense of freedom soar. Double
mat enlarged photo on black and white
cardstocks; adhere letter pebbles (Creative
Imaginations) at bottom of photo. Crop
three photos into squares; mat on black
cardstock. Mount all photos on preprinted
color-blocked paper (SEI).

Martha Crowther, Salem, New Hampshire

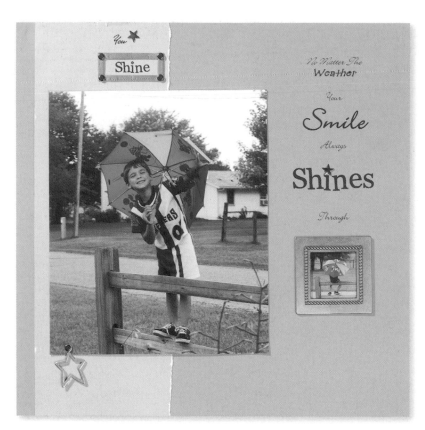

You Shine

Not even gloomy weather can dampen the playful and charismatic personality of Renae's son. Print title and journaling on gray and blue papers. Slice a 4" strip of gray paper; tear one edge and mount on blue paper background. Attach silver frame around one title word with small brads. Mount enlarged photo on page; attach star charm (Making Memories) at bottom of page with small silver brad. Mount cropped photo behind metal frame (Making Memories). Mount blue metal stars (Scrapyard 329) around title and journaling.

Renae Clark, Mazomanie, Wisconsin

Ripples Of Fun

A shallow puddle provides hours of enjoyment at the end of a rainy day for Brooke's little boy. Cut two 5¼" squares of mustard cardstock; mount at bottom of blue cardstock and patterned paper (Far and Away) backgrounds. Emboss gold brads (Office Depot) with blue embossing powder; attach blue brads at outside corners of mustard cardstock squares. Slice one 2" and two 1" strips of patterned paper; vertically and horizontally mount on left page as shown. Repeat with blue cardstock; mount on right page. Adhere title letters (Club Scrap) at top of left page. Mount cropped photos along bottom of both pages. Mat one photo on mustard cardstock; mount at top of right page. Write journaling on vellum with blue pen; cut to size and attach to page with blue brads. Adhere one letter sticker on right page; write balance of name and date with blue pen.

Brooke Sparks, Louisville, Kentucky

Why Do Boys Love Snakes?

Living in the country gives Chris' son many opportunities to nurture his fascination with nature and creatures that live in the grass. Layer patterned paper (KI Memories) over blue cardstock for background. Slice a 2½" strip of white cardstock; mat on green cardstock; mount near top of left page. Print title and journaling on green, white and blue cardstocks. Tear around edges of title words on green cardstock; mount at top of left page and bottom of right page. Silhouette cut large title words printed on blue and green cardstocks; layer letter "s" over small green cardstock frame. Mount glass pebble (Making Memories) over one title word; attach screw eyelets (Making Memories) on torn green cardstock with title words. Punch frog (McGill) from green cardstock; mount with title at bottom of right page. Double mat one photo on two shades of green cardstock slightly askew; mount at right of title on left page. Mount cropped photos on green cardstock tags; wrap top of tag with string. Punch and re-punch circles from green cardstock; mount at top of tags. Cut journaling block and strips to size; single and double mat journaling on blue and green cardstocks.

Chris Douglas, East Rochester, Ohio

Who Needs Toys...?

A little boy can keep busy and happy digging in the dirt with sticks, leaving his mother to wonder about the value of a room full of toys. Mat green cardstock with navy blue cardstock. Single and double mat photos on white and navy blue cardstocks. Print title, journaling and quote on green cardstock; cut to size and mat on navy blue cardstock. Attach eyelets at corners of one double-matted photo; frame photo with fibers (Fibers By The Yard). String fibers through eyelets and secure at back of page. Mount stitched green square buttons (Making Memories) on silver-rimmed tags (Making Memories). Attach silver eyelet and tie with fibers.

Kenna Ewing, Parkside, Pennsylvania

Logan

Beth uses descriptive words to accompany photos of her son exploring an outdoor campsite. Dampen, crumple and flatten brown cardstock; when dry, brush with green and brown chalks for extra dimension and shading. Mat distressed cardstock on brown cardstock brushed with sandpaper. Wrap fibers (On The Surface) around bottom of matted cardstock background; dangle leaf buttons (Jesse James) from fibers. Mat two photos on dark green cardstock; rub sandpaper on matting. Wrap fibers around bottom of one matted photo; dangle leaf buttons from fibers. Layer photos on page; mount two photos with self-adhesive foam spacers. Print title and descriptive words on vellum; crop around words and mount alongside photos.

Beth Rogers, Mesa, Arizona

Perhaps Imagination Is Intelligence

Renae documents an average day of play in the life of three 6-year-olds. Tear ½" and 2½" strips of tan cardstock. Tear, crumple and flatten green paper; layer with tan cardstock strips at top and bottom of brown cardstock background. Mount gray and pewter leaf eyelets (Making Memories) at corners of torn paper strips. Mat two photos on one piece of green cardstock. Print title and journaling on tan cardstock; tear edges and mat on green cardstock. Tear around largest title word and mat on dark brown cardstock; layer on title block with distressed green paper scrap, pewter leaf eyelet and small green leaf button (Jesse James). Mount silver photo corners (Making Memories) on matted journaling block. Tie fiber around pewter leaf plaque (Making Memories); layer with matted photo on distressed green paper.

Renae Clark, Mazomanie, Wisconsin

Worm Hunting

Denise's young grandson lost interest in gardening when he developed a serious fascination with earthworms buried in the dirt. Double mat photo on brown and red cardstocks for left page. Tear five 1" strips of dark brown cardstock; brush torn edges with brown chalk for dimension and layer at top of left and bottom of right pages. Cut title words from brown cardstock using templates (C-Thru Ruler). Layer large title letters in front of and behind torn cardstock strips. Punch ash leaves and ferns (Punch Bunch) from two shades of green cardstock; nestle amongst brown torn cardstock strips on both pages. Print journaling on tan cardstock; tear edges and detail with brown chalk. Mat two photos together on red cardstock.

Denise DeYoung, Windsor, Ontario, Canada

Jake, 6

Josh's Room

Josh feels like a very big boy in his new room and loves having a space to call his own. Print title and journaling on yellow and red cardstocks. Slice three ¼" strips of black cardstock; vertically mount two strips on both sides of title as shown. Crop two title letters printed on red cardstock; mount in place with small green brads (Karen Foster Design). Mat photos on black cardstock. Embellish one photo mat with small red squares, green and black brads (Karen Foster Design) and a thin strip of yellow cardstock. Horizontally mount third ¼" black strip at center of both pages. Complete page with small green brads mounted atop small black squares.

Kim Haynes, Harrah, Oklahoma

Keep On Truckin'

A little boy's fascination with trucks grows when he experiences the freedom of roaming the neighborhood sidewalks with his first set of wheels. Mount dark blue cardstock and blue mesh (Magic Mesh) over white cardstock background. Print title and journaling on red, yellow, green and white cardstocks. Crop red, yellow and green printed cardstocks into circles to fit inside silver-rimmed circle tags (Making Memories). Crop photo to fit inside square silver-rimmed tag (Making Memories); mount all tags on mesh at top of page. Cut journaling to size; mat on yellow cardstock. Punch state shape (EK Success) from white cardstock; mount on punched red squares (Emagination Crafts).

Jennifer Miller, Humble, Texas

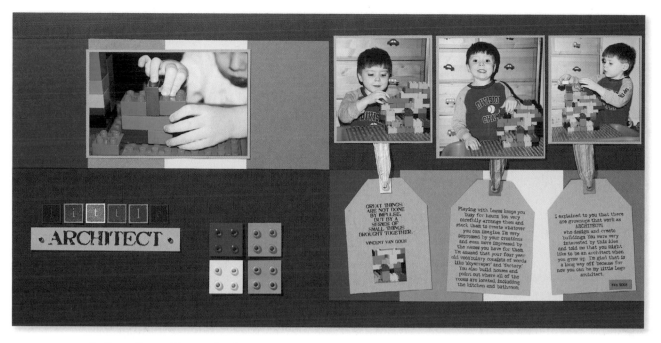

Little Architect

Amber's son spends hours arranging, stacking and constructing detailed buildings and bridges with oodles of Lego blocks and even more imagination. Cut two 2⅞ x 5" pieces of these colored cardstocks: red, blue, yellow and green. Horizontally mount in a row on black cardstock pages as shown. Print part of title, journaling and quote on tan cardstock. Cut title word into a strip; mount on black background with small silver brads (Stamp Doctor). Stamp first title word (Hero Arts) with colored inks; cut to size and mount above word strip. Crop quote and journaling into tag shapes; attach colored eyelet over small colored square at top of tag. Tie with matching colored paper yarn (Emagination Crafts, Making Memories). Crop photo into small square; mount under quote on tag. Mat photos on tan cardstock. Punch four 1¼" squares from colored cardstocks; attach same-colored eyelets on squares to resemble Lego building blocks.

Amber Crosby, Houston, Texas

Lessons From Ty

Denise successfully captures unique characteristics that make her 4-year-old "all boy." Begin with a matted background. Mat enlargement and mount with self-adhesive foam spacers onto torn, corrugated paper (MPR Associates) mat. In a word-processing program, type journaling in white text on black, fill-in background and print. Cut words or phrases apart to look like label-maker strips. Mount journaling on textured papers (Creative Imaginations), mat and add small matted photos. Finish page by adding stamped and beaded tags (Making Memories) and heart charm (Boutique Trims).

Denise Tucker, Versailles, Indiana

Captain Underpants

Cheryl uses color-blocking to turn her son's interesting headgear and boyish characteristics into a popular children's book series. Computer-print a portion of journaling across top of background paper. Computer-print title and remainder of journaling on complementary-colored cardstock; trim into panels or blocks and mount in place on background. Finish with cropped photos and lettered beads (Wal-Mart).

Cheryl Overton, Kelowna, British Columbia, Canada

It Is A Happy Talent

Stacy's children have a knack for knowing how to play and explore for hours on end at a nearby park. Print title on red cardstock and blue patterned paper (Doodlebug Design). Silhouette and reverse-cut title letters from blue patterned paper; crop blue paper into circle using circle cutter or template, slicing through any letters if necessary. Crop three more circles from blue patterned paper. Layer mustard cardstock, circles and photos over red cardstock for a graphic background. Crop one photo into circle. Mount alphabet and heart beads (Crafts Etc.) on photos. Complete page with name and date written with black pen.

Stacy McFadden, Doncaster East, Victoria, Australia

The Hat

Chris tells the story of a very special and meaningful birthday gift her son is rarely seen without. Create a color-blocked background with pieces of white, red and tan cardstocks. Print part of title, date and journaling on tan, red and white cardstocks. Cut journaling block; rub black inkpad over edges of white cardstock before mounting on page. Silhouette cut title word on tan cardstock; mount above journaling. Attach metal letter eyelets on red strip at top of page. Cut date strip to size; attach to page with pewter flat eyelet (Making Memories). Mount baseball preprinted image (Leeco) on red square matted with black cardstock. Cut a piece of red cardstock larger than photo; brush with modeling paste (Liquitex). When dry, attach large rivets (Chatterbox) at corners. Mount photo with glue dots over textured matting; mount at center of page.

Chris Douglas, East Rochester, Ohio

I Feel The Need For Speed

Leave it to a little boy with a huge imagination to have fun in a car that doesn't even run! Cut a 3" strip of scrap metal (Once Upon a Scribble); mount at left side of black cardstock. Print title and journaling on red cardstock. Cut journaling block to size; layer on metal strip and mount metal letter eyelet (Making Memories). Double mat photo on black and red cardstocks. Cut photo corners from scrap metal; attach large silver eyelets (Creative Imaginations) and small brads (Making Memories) on each photo corner. Cut title and date on red cardstock into strips; mount below photo as shown.

Tamara Morrison, Trabuco Canyon, California

A Boy and His Lawnmower

Rhonda watches her little boy enjoy his weekly lawnmower ride. To re-create this computer-generated layout, (Microsoft Picture It!) first create background by experimenting with various textures and techniques provided by software program. Scan in actual buttons and type letters atop button images. Scan actual frames (Making Memories) to use as placeholder in digital layout, then place actual frames over images when computer layout is complete. Create large frame by elongating square shapes; add "brads" by creating tan circles and add texture for dimension. Add text to layout in desired fonts to finish. To create layout manually, first print journaling and date on green cardstock. Mount a tan cardstock strip and green gingham cardstock strip at left and right sides of green cardstock background. Mat large photo on page; slice four ¼" strips of green cardstock and mount slightly askew around large photo as shown. Attach large brad fasteners at strip intersections. Write partial title on tan cardstock strip. Adhere letter stickers on textured cardstock circles. Mount metal frames over small photos.

Rhonda Altus, Walnut Grove, Missouri

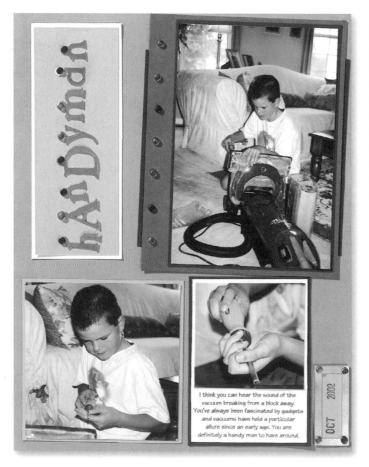

Handyman

Lisa's scrapbook page pays homage to her little handyman, who "seems to hear the vacuum breaking from a block away." Computer-print journaling onto cardstock. Crop and mat photos, matting one on trimmed journaling; mount on page. Create title with brad fasteners and metal letters (Making Memories). Stamp date (Avery) and layer behind metal tag (Making Memories) with brad fasteners.

Lisa Simon, Granville, Ohio

Jake, 6 and Dakota

Camo Gear

Nancy's son celebrates a "coming-of-age" birthday gift that links privilege with responsibility. Mount photos on dark green cardstock. Print title and journaling on vellum; cut to size and mat on brown cardstock. Attach silver eyelets (Making Memories) at bottom corners of vellum. Tear patterned paper corner (The Paper Company) and punch maple leaves (EK Success) from green and brown cardstocks; layer both at top of title/journaling block. Re-create camouflage netting with a black lightweight fabric; attach at upper left corner with silver eyelets. Punch leaves from orange, brown and green cardstocks; mount atop fabric as shown.

Nancy McCoy, Gulfport, Mississippi

Army Men

Pam pays homage to the depth of her boys' creative play with great photos of classic boy toys—army men! Begin by mounting a green cardstock block on a tan background. Add strips of camouflaged burlap for borders across top and side of background. Crop and adhere photos. Add letter stickers (SEI) to create title. Computer print journaling in desired font onto vellum; adhere to side border with brad fasteners (Making Memories). Finish page with additional brad fasteners along lower edge of page.

Pam Canavan, Clermont, Florida

Boy And Dog

Maryann captures the close relationship between her son and his dog on a simple layout with warm colors. Print title and journaling on mustard cardstock background. Mat two photos on taupe cardstock; mount on page with a 1¼" strip of taupe cardstock. Adhere sticker flowers and squares (C-Thru Ruler) on photo mat and taupe cardstock strip and squares. Mat flower sticker squares.

Maryann Wise, Bakersfield, California

Sunflower Seed

A young boy revels in the fact that he finally gets a pet to take care of and call his own. Slice two 1¼" strips of orange cardstock; tear one edge and mount at top and bottom of brown mulberry paper (Artistic Scrapper). Print title and journaling on orange cardstock; mount between torn strips. Single and double mat photos on brown and taupe cardstocks; mount around title and text, tucking top of one photo under torn strip. Mount black buttons (Hillcreek Designs).

Dee Gallimore-Perry, Griswold, Connecticut

Nature

The smallest and simplest aspects of nature can capture the curiosity of a little boy. Tear a 1" strip of green cardstock; vertically mount with strands of raffia as a border at left side of left page. Print descriptive words and journaling on vellum. Tear around descriptive words; layer on torn brown cardstock scraps. Mount with copper eyelets and layer on border strip. Mat photos on tan, brown and green cardstocks with torn edges. Embellish matting with copper eyelets. String raffia through two eyelets and tie over photo on left page. Cut title letters from brown cardstock using template (Frances Meyer). Tear top and bottom edges of journaling block. Punch squares (McGill) from brown crumpled and flattened cardstock. Mount textured squares at left of journaling block and at bottom of right page. Stamp leaf designs (Hero Arts) on tan cardstock; cut into tag shape and tie with raffia. Detail leaves with green and brown chalks.

Valerie Barton, Flowood, Mississippi

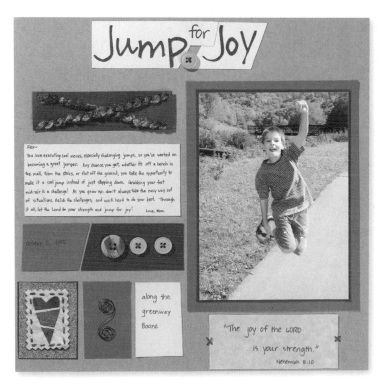

Jump For Joy

Patty's son loves to execute cool moves, especially challenging jumps from a bench, down the stairs or flat off the ground. Double mat photo on brown and green cardstocks. Print title on brown cardstock; silhouette cut and mount on ivory cardstock. Cut title word strips on an angle as shown; mount stitched button. Pierce holes at corners of brown cardstock strip; crisscross fibers (Lion Brand) and feed through holes. Journal on ivory cardstock; cut to size. Cut green and brown cardstock strips; slice on an angle at one end. Mount buttons on brown strip. Crop preprinted accent (EK Success); mat on brown cardstock. Twist brass wire (Artistic Wire) into curled "S" shape; mount on green cardstock. Write location details on ivory cardstock with brown pen. Print quote on vellum strip; stitch to page with brown thread (DMC).

Patty Browne, Boone, North Carolina

The Boy on His Bike

Harley Davidson is the sign of this Boy on his Bike. His companion and friend, carrying him far and wide, This Boy on his Bike. The wind whistling past his ears, ruffling the long hair on his head, Taking him on long excursions into the wilderness of vast stretches of road. This Boy on his Bike.
AJ Allen

The Boy On His Bike

A toddler gets his first taste of riding down the open road with the wind in his hair on a Harley of his own. Print title and journaling on vellum; cut to size and mount at top of left page with motorcycle logo. Attach large eyelets (Making Memories) at top corners of vellum. Add texture to black cardstock: dampen, crumple, flatten and then iron. Mat two photos on black textured paper; cut photo corners and squares from black textured paper. Mount cropped photos behind red slide mounts (source unknown). Punch small holes at insides of two 2¾" squares. Score and fold outside edges to create the flap openings; adhere only outside edges and lace with black fibers (Fibers By The Yard); mount outside edges with large silver eyelets. Embellish photo mats and corners, slide mounts and decorative squares with rhinestones (JewelCraft). Adhere letter stickers (Deluxe Designs) on metal dog tag (JewelCraft); mount on page with chain.

Wendy Bickford, Antelope, California

Magnet Man

Shannon captures the fascination on her son's face as he tries to figure out the magic of a magnet. Print journaling on white cardstock; mat on red cardstock. Layer blue and yellow plastic letters (Heidi Grace Designs) with photos. Mount real magnets (Dowling Magnets) or small metal-rimmed tags along bottom of page.

Shannon Taylor, Bristol, Tennessee

Boys At Play

Renae's photos exemplify boys' playful spirits and zest for life. Slice a 2¾" strip of red paper; mount at bottom of blue paper. Flatten paper yarn (Making Memories); horizontally mount at top of red strip. Print part of title and names on patterned paper (Mustard Moon). Mat photos on red paper. Mount silver photo corners (Making Memories) on one photo; layer on patterned paper. Attach silver metal letters (Making Memories) on silver-rimmed tags (Making Memories) with red and blue eyelets. Mount on flattened paper yarn layered over patterned paper. Attach metal star eyelets (Making Memories) at ends of paper yarn. Mount small photo behind silver frame (Making Memories). Cut names on patterned paper to size; mount on page with colored eyelets.

Renae Clark, Mazomanie, Wisconsin

Under Construction

A little boy is a work in progress. Tear brown paper pieces; brush edges with brown chalk. Layer on matted orange background (Karen Foster Design) to look like dirt hills. Adhere truck and cone stickers (me & my BIG ideas) on white cardstock; silhouette cut. Layer on page with torn brown paper. Mat one photo on brown paper (Karen Foster Design); layer over textured handmade paper (source unknown) and vellum with torn edges. Stamp title (Stampin' Up!) and part of quote with brown ink; write balance of title with brown pen. Crop circle to fit inside metal-rimmed tag (Making Memories); attach orange eyelet and tie with fiber (EK Success). Hang from corner of photo.

Suzy Plantamura for me & my BIG ideas, Laguna Niguel, California

Taking A Drink

Trying to drink from a cool stream of water is a challenging—and drenching—experience for Kristin's son. Mat three photos together on white cardstock; mount at right side of blue cardstock background. Print title and journaling on orange and white cardstocks. Slice orange, navy blue and green cardstocks in varying widths; horizontally mount on white cardstock with journaling to look like stripe design on shirt. Mat photo on striped cardstock above journaling. Cut title strip to size; attach to matted photo with square clip (Making Memories).

Kristin Baxter, Houston, Texas

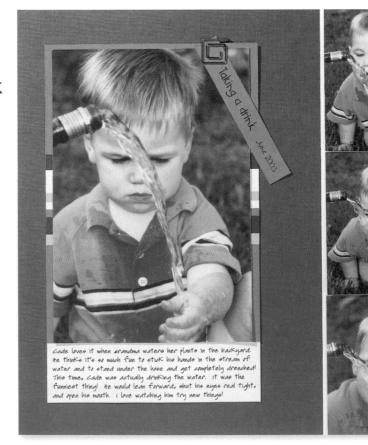

Pure Boy

Leave it to a couple of boys to want to keep any kind of crawling creature they pick up off the ground. Using a ruler and craft knife, slice three windows in vellum; vertically tear left edge of vellum. Layer vellum and photos on patterned paper (Cut-It-Up). Print large title words on vellum; cut into strip and mount between photos. Mount glass pebble on letter "O." Write balance of title and journaling on vellum with black pen. Craft a journaled shaker box: cut a 2¾ x 1½" window in a 3¼ x 2" piece of tan cardstock. Mount a 3 x 1¾" piece of transparency or clear page protector behind window. Adhere foam tape around back of window frame; mount over journaling block and seal with rocks inside. Embellish outside of shaker box with mosaic tiles (Magic Scraps). Attach spiral clips (Target) to vellum; mount bronze turtles (source unknown) on clips.

Ruthann Grabowski, Yorktown, Virginia

Inquire, Inspect, Investigate

A muddy puddle provides a pool of creative adventures and hours of enjoyment for Rhonda's two boys. Add visual interest to a computer-generated layout (Microsoft Picture It!) by starting with a textured background. Scan and use patterned paper squares as placeholders in computer layout, adding physical paper squares atop scanned images. Layer journaling text in desired font atop layout to complete. Re-create this layout with patterned paper squares (Creative Imaginations, Karen Foster Design, The Paper Patch) layered with photos atop orange cardstock background. Adhere letter stickers for title. Print journaling on ivory cardstock; cut to size and mount at bottom of page.

Rhonda Altus, Walnut Grove, Missouri
Inspiration: Shannon Freeman,
Bellingham, Washington

G.I. Austin

With just a bit of face paint and some camouflage gear, a young "soldier" enlists himself in his own army. Print journaling and name on ivory cardstock; cut journaling block to size and tear edges. Brush torn edges with brown and green chalks. Cut "Army" letters from pre-printed paper (Hot Off The Press); attach silver eyelets. Adhere number stickers (Provo Craft) on metal tag (Making Memories). Assemble photos, printed tag (Hot Off The Press), silver beaded chain and tag, metal letter tiles (Making Memories) and journaling block layered on mesh paper. Collage all pieces on patterned paper (Karen Foster Design) background. Attach silver star brad fasteners (Creative Impressions). Tear a 9" square window from brown cardstock and a 9½" square window from patterned paper (Karen Foster Design). Layer atop another and brush torn edges with brown and green chalks. Gently curl torn edges away from center. Mount layers on 8½" foam core frame; adhere frame atop collage. Attach star brad over ivory strip with printed name on frame.

Cheryl Uribe, Grapevine, Texas

Doggone Good Friends

A gentle and faithful golden retriever is the perfect wrestling partner for Kelly's rambunctious son. Slice a 4½" strip of patterned paper (Cut-It-Up); mount at top of black cardstock. Tear red, blue and white cardstock strips; brush edges with tan and brown chalks and layer at center of page. Cut title letters from patterned paper using template (EK Success); mat on black cardstock and silhouette cut. Freehand cut bones from brown cardstock; detail with pen and brown chalk. Stamp title letters (Hero Arts) with black ink. Paper piece dog and doghouse from pre-made pattern (Bumper Crops) on red, brown and black cardstocks. Print journaling; cut to size and mount on patterned paper. Mat two photos together on white cardstock; double mat on green or blue cardstocks.

Kelly Angard, Highlands Ranch, Colorado

Silly Little Shaver

Kelly's son has quite a bit of good, clean fun with a can of shaving cream and toy razor. Crop two photos into ovals; double mat on blue paper and textured fleece paper. Crop another photo with decorative scissors; double mat and trim with decorative scissors. Cut title from fleece paper using template (Provo Craft); mount across patterned paper (Making Memories) background. Silhouette cut photo on left page. Freehand draw can of shaving cream; paper piece from silver, red and black cardstocks and vellum. Adhere black letter stickers (Making Memories), outline and write details with black pen. Freehand cut mounds of shaving cream from fleece paper; shade with gray chalk. Using a shape cutter, crop oval at bottom of large shaving cream mound. Mount photo behind oval window.

Kelly Angard, Highlands Ranch, Colorado

A Driver's Lesson

A young man's first day behind the wheel of his dad's treasured Corvette proves to be a lesson in high anxiety! Divide white cardstock into quadrants for color-blocked background. Cut red patterned papers (Provo Craft) and black cardstock to fit quadrants. Print part of title and journaling on red and white cardstocks. Double and triple mat smaller photos on black, red and white cardstocks and patterned paper (source unknown). Slice journaling sentences on white cardstock into strips; mount at bottom of small matted photos on right side of page. Mat three photos on one piece of black cardstock; layer with silver metal mesh (AMACO). Ink and collage white cardstock with solid and patterned papers. Cut into tag shapes using template (Deluxe Designs); attach eyelets. Layer cropped journaling over metal mesh scraps on tags. Mount journaling tags at left of large photos. Cut letter "A" from white cardstock using template (Scrap Pagerz); emboss with silver powder and set with heat gun. Silhouette cut title letters printed on red paper; brush with black and silver inks before mounting on patterned paper strip. Mount letter strip on page with self-adhesive foam spacers. Adhere letter stickers (Creative Imaginations) for third title word.

Kelly Angard, Highlands Ranch, Colorado

Page Title Ideas

If writer's block prevents you from thinking of page titles that speak to the heart of your photos, use these convenient page title ideas for inspiration. Create your own handmade or computer-generated page titles for a custom-coordinated, designer look. For added sizzle, accent page titles with theme-appropriate stickers, die cuts, punched shapes, colorants or embellishments.

Attitude Is Everything

A hair-raising experience
A laugh is a grin that has burst
A magic spirit
Aim high
Be yourself
Being a boy is cause enough for celebration
Boy meets world
Determination
Don't mess with me
Every girl's crazy about a sharp-dressed man!
He man
Hooked on you
I believe I can fly
I believe in you
I'm a keeper
Just plain cute
King of the castle
Knight in shining armor
Like a rock
Love the skin you're in!
Of all the animals, the boy is the most unmanageable
One hot kid
Silly boy
Sometimes it's best to just let what's in you come out
Stuck in the middle with you
Success is loving life and daring to live it
Such a boy!
That's my boy!
The many faces of…
Today you are you. That is truer than true. There is no one alive who is You-er than you! –Dr. Seuss
Top son
True grit
Uniquely you
What a guy!
What's the buzz?
Yeah, me bad

Deep thoughts
Delight in the little things
Denim daydreams
Every rough and tumble boy has a soft side
Follow your dreams, wherever they may lead you
God gives us faces, we create our own expressions
Hand in hand, man to man
Handsome
Hang on to your boyhood as long as you can!
He ain't heavy, he's my brother
He wears his heart in his smile
Imagination is more important than knowledge
It's the merry-hearted boys that make the best men
Joy of my life
Little boy, big hugs
Live, laugh, love
Love understands love, it needs no talk
Love unmeasurable
May you never lose your sense of wonder
Moments of solitude
My guy
My little boy
My prince
My son, my joy, my love, my life
Nothing is so strong as gentleness between brothers
Our angel
Our dream for you
Our sun
See the wisdom of the ages, but look at the world through the eyes of a child
Simple pleasures, priceless treasures
Slow down, little man
Smitten with a kitten
Sometimes being a brother is even better than being a superhero
Summer child
Sweet baby face
Sweet little boy
Take time to smell the roses
Teetering on the edge between babyhood and boyhood
The joy is in the journey, not the destination
Time together lasts forever
To the world you are one person, but to this person, you are the world
Today a boy, tomorrow a man

The Softer Side

A boy is a joy
American sweetheart
Between the innocence of babyhood and the dignity of manhood, we find a delightful creature of a boy
Blissful boyhood moments
Boys are treasures
Can you see me now?

What I love about you…
When you were born…
Where are you going?
You are a miracle
You are incomparable
You are my sunshine
You hold the key to my heart
You steal my heart away

It's A Boy's Life

A boy of many hats
A little dirt never hurt
Boy, a noise with dirt on it
Boy inside and out
Boy style
Boy time
Boys at play
Boys at work
Boyz rule!
Built strong
Bundle of energy
Fly-boy
Game boy
Game time
Hockey (any sport) legend
It is a happy talent to know how to play
It's a boy's life
It's a guy thing
Jump for joy
Just an ordinary boy who does extraordinary things
Lord of the rings
Our fall guy
Play
Play ball
Proud to be a boy
Pure boy
Put me in coach, I'm ready to play
Ready to rumble
Ride the wind
Take flight
The boys' club
The need for speed
Weekend warrior
What a catch
Wild thing, you make my heart sing
You're an all star
You're one in a million

Boys Will Be Boys

100% boy
A boy and his dog
A boy and his toy
A boy is…
A dad, a boy and their toy
An adventure should be adventurous
Beach boy
Born to be wild
Boy genius
Boy unruly
Boys, boys, boys
Boys only
Boys will be boys
Buddy boys
Clowning around
Creepy crawlers
Daddy's boy
Dripping dudes
Hanging out
Here comes trouble
I dig dirt
I smile because you're my brother, I laugh because you can't
    do a thing about it
Just boys being boys
Just like dad
Lil' partner
Little boy on the prairie
Little boys' pockets hold…
Look what I did
Man in training
Me and my toad
Mechanic in training
Meet Joe Dirt
Modern primitive
Monkeyin' around
Mountain man
My favorite handyman
Nature boy
No girls allowed
Oh boy
Oh brother
Rite of passage
Snakes alive!
Snakes, snails and puppy-dog tails
Soldier boy
The cat and her boy
The dog and his boy
The foreman
The road to maturity
The world is mud-licious and puddle-wonderful.
    —E.E. Cummings
There's a little cowboy in all of us—a little frontier
What are little boys made of?
You want a piece of me?

Additional Instructions & Credits

COVER

Photocopy and enlarge page from an old dictionary; tear top and bottom edges before layering on blue background. Slice a strip of yellow vellum large enough to cover "boy" definition on copy; mount with clear adhesive. Double mat photo on white and blue cardstocks; tear bottom of second matting. Color brass drawer plate (source unknown) with silver paint pen (Krylon). Print title on white cardstock; cut to size and mount behind silver drawer plate. Tie yellow ribbon (Offray) to sides of drawer plate; secure at top of page. Dangle silver charms (JewelCraft) on spiral clips (Boxer Scrapbook Productions); attach to page and photo mat as shown.

Betsy Bell Sammarco, New Canaan, Connecticut

PAGE 1 THE BEST THINGS ABOUT BEING A BOY

Double mat photo on yellow cardstock and patterned vellum (Stampin' Up!). Slice a 1" strip of patterned vellum; mount on page with small yellow brads (HyGlo/American Pin). Die cut title letters (QuiKutz) from yellow cardstock; mount at top of page. Die cut window tags (QuicKutz) from patterned vellum. Print captions on yellow cardstock; crop to fit behind window tags. Mount on page with small yellow brads.

Jodi Amidei, Memory Makers; Photo: MaryJo Regier, Memory Makers

PAGE 3 BOOKPLATE

Using ½", ¾" and 1" square punches (EK Success, Emagination Crafts, Family Treasures), punch sports ball stickers (EK Success). Layer at left side of page using self-adhesive foam spacers for dimension alongside a ¼" sliced basketball image frame. Use this idea in different themes that correspond with photos of your boy's favorite activities.

Jodi Amidei, Memory Makers

PAGE 6 BIONICLE BOY

Begin with blue matted tan background. Cut apart patterned paper (Chatterbox) following design lines; adhere along edges of background. Layer photos and adhere. Sprinkle embossing powder on coin mounts (Whitman Publishing); set with a heat embossing gun. Adhere coin mounts on page as desired using self-adhesive foam spacers on some, and filling centers with toys or backing openings with additional photos. Finish page with embossed, die-cut letters (QuicKutz) for title and computer-printed, matted journaling.

Michele Gerbrandt, Memory Makers; Photos: Ken Trujillo, Memory Makers

PAGE 7 HOOPS

Layer patterned paper strip (Paper Loft) over blue background (Bazzill). Stamp basketball-related words with letter stamps (Hero Arts, PSX Design, Rubber Stampeded, Stampin' Up!) in white ink. Apply "hoops" title in upper left corner with self-adhesive foam spacers. Apply black embossing powder (Ranger) to quarter-, half-circle and ¼" wide straight paper strips; heat set and adhere to page to mimic basketball court markings. Crop and mat photos; adhere. Computer-print journaling, scuff up with ink pad; adhere. Finish with game ticket memorabilia and dimensional stickers (Jolee's Boutique).

Jodi Amidei, Memory Makers; Photos: MaryJo Regier, Memory Maker

PAGE 33 DENNIS THE MENACE

Dennis the Menace created by Hank Ketcham © 2002 North America Syndicate. © North America Syndicate and Cowles Syndicate are affiliated companies of King Features Syndicate, a unit of The Hearst Corporation.

Artist Index

Photo Credits

Sources

The following companies manufacture products featured in this book. Please check your local retailers to find these materials, or go to a company's Web site for the latest product. In addition, we have made every attempt to properly credit the items mentioned in this book. We apologize to any company that we have listed incorrectly, and we would appreciate hearing from you.

3M Stationary
(800) 364-3577
www.3m.com

7gypsies™
(800) 588-6707
www.7gypsies.com

Adobe
www.adobe.com

All My Memories
(888) 553-1998
www.allmymemories.com

All Night Media
(see Plaid Enterprises, Inc.)

American Art Clay Co.,
AMACO
(800) 374-1600
www.amaco.com

American Crafts
(800) 879-5185
www.ultimatepens.com

American Tag Company
(800) 223-3956
www.americantag.net

Amscan, Inc.
(800) 444-8887
www.amscan.com

Artistic Scrapper
(818) 786-8304
www.artisticscrapper.com

Artistic Wire Ltd.™
(630) 530-7567
www.artisticwire.com

Autumn Leaves
(wholesale only)
(800) 588-6707
www.autumnleaves.com

Avery Dennison Corporation
www.avery.com

Bo Bunny Press
(801) 771-4010
www.bobunny.com

Boutique Trims, Inc.
(248) 437-4017
www.boutiquetrims.com

Boxer Scrapbook Productions
(503) 625-0455
www.boxerscrapbooks.com

Brown Bag Fibers
no contact info. available

Bumper Crops
(615) 696-1552

ChartPak
(800) 628-1910
www.chartpak.com

Chatterbox, Inc.
(888) 416-6260
www.chatterboxinc.com

Chronicle Books
www.chroniclebooks.com

Clearsnap, Inc.
(360) 293-6634
www.clearsnap.com

Close To My Heart®
(888) 655-6552
www.closetomyheart.com

Club Scrap™, Inc.
(888) 634-9100
www.clubscrap.com

Colorbök™, Inc
(wholesale only)
(800) 366-4660
www.colorbok.com

Craf-T Products
(507) 235-3996
www.craf-tproducts.com

Crafter's Workshop, The
(877) CRAFTER
www.thecraftersworkshop.com

Crafts, Etc. Ltd.
(800) 888-0321
www.craftsetc.com

Creative Imaginations
(wholesale only)
(800) 942-6487
www.cigift.com

Creative Impressions
(719) 577-4858
www.creativeimpressions.com

Creative Memories®
(800) 468-9335
www.creativememories.com

C-Thru® Ruler Company, The
(wholesale only)
(800) 243-8419
www.cthruruler.com

Cut-It-Up™
(530) 389-2233
www.cut-it-up.com

Darice, Inc.
(800) 321-1494
www.darice.com

DayCo Ltd.
(877) 595-8160
www.daycodiecuts.com

Debbie Mumm®
(888) 819-2923
www.debbiemumm.com

Deluxe Designs
(480) 497-9005
www.deluxecuts.com

Design Originals
(800) 877-7820
www.d originals.com

DMC Corp.
(973) 589-0606
www.dmc-usa.com

DMD Industries, Inc.
(800) 805-9890
www.dmdind.com

Doodlebug Design, Inc.™
(801) 966-9952
www.doodlebugdesigninc.com

Dowling Magnets
(800) MAGNET-1
www.dowlingmagnets.com

Duncan Enterprises
(559) 291-4444
www.duncancrafts.com

EK Success™ ,Ltd. (wholesale only)
(800) 524-1349
www.eksuccess.com

Emagination Crafts, Inc.
(630) 833-9521
www.emaginationcrafts.com

Family Treasures, Inc.®
www.familytreasures.com

Far And Away
(509) 340-0124
www.farandawayscrapbooks.com

Faux Memories
(813) 269-7946
www.fauxmemories.com

Fibers By The Yard
(800) 760-8901
www.fibersbytheyard.com

Fiskars, Inc.
(800) 950-0203
www.fiskars.com

FooFaLa
(402) 758-0863
www.foofala.com

Frances Meyer, Inc.®
(800) 372-6237
www.francesmeyer.com

Freckle Press
(877) 4-FRECKL
www.frecklepress.com

Hampton Art Stamps
(800) 229-1019
www.hamptonart.com

Hancock Fabrics
www.hancockfabrics.com

Happy Hammer, The
(303) 690-3883
www.thehappyhammer.com

Hasbro
www.hasbro.com

Heidi Grace Designs
(253) 735-9008
www.heidigrace.com

Hemera Technologies, Inc.
(819) 772-8200
www.hemera.com

Hero Arts® Rubber Stamps, Inc.
(800) 822-4376
www.heroarts.com

Hewlett Packard
www.hp.com

Hillcreek Designs
(619) 562-5799
www.hillcreekdesigns.com

Hot Off The Press, Inc.
(800) 227-9595
www.paperpizazz.com

Hyglo®/American Pin
(800) 821-7125
www.americanpin.com

Impress Rubber Stamps
(206) 901-9101
www.impressrubberstamps.com

Impression Obsession
(877) 259-0905
www.impression-obsession.com

Inkadinkado® Rubber Stamps
(800) 888-4652
www.inkadinkado.com

Jesse James & Co., Inc.
(610) 435-0201
www.jessejamesbutton.com

JewelCraft, LLC
(201) 223-0804
www.jewelcraft.biz

Karen Foster Design™
(wholesale only)
(801) 451-9779
www.karenfosterdesign.com

KI Memories
(469) 633-9665
www.kimemories.com

Krylon
(216) 515-7693
www.krylon.com

Lasting Impressions for Paper, Inc.
(801) 298-1979
www.lastingimpressions.com

Leave Memories
www.leavememories.com

Leeco Industries, Inc.
(800) 826-8806
www.leecoindustries.com

Lego
www.lego.com

Li'l Davis Designs
(949) 838-0344
www.lildavisdesigns.com

Limited Edition Rubberstamps
(650) 299-9700
www.limitededitionrs.com

Lion Brand Yarn Company
www.lionbrandyarn.com

Liquitex Artist Materials
(888) 4-ACRYLIC
www.liquitex.com

Lost Art Treasures-
no contact info. available

Magenta Rubber Stamps
(800) 565-5254
www.magentarubberstamps.com

Magic Mesh™
(651) 345-6374
www.magicmesh.com

Magic Scraps™
(972) 238-1838
www.magicscraps.com

Making Memories
(800) 286-5263
www.makingmemories.com

Manto Fev
www.mantofev.com

Martha Stewart
(800) 950-7130
www.marthastewart.com

Marvy® Uchida
(wholesale only)
(800) 541-5877
www.uchida.com

McGill Inc.
(800) 982-9884
www.mcgillinc.com

me & my BIG ideas
(949) 589-4607
www.meandmybigideas.com

Microsoft
www.microsoft.com

MJ Designs
no contact info. available

MPR Associates, Inc.
(336) 861-6343

Mrs. Grossman's Paper Co.
(wholesale only)
(800) 429-4549
www.mrsgrossmans.com

Mustard Moon™ Paper
(408) 229-8542
www.mustardmoon.com

My Mind's Eye™, Inc.
(801) 298-3709
www.frame-ups.com

Nova Development Corporation
(818) 591-9600
www.novadevelopment.com

NRN Designs
(800) 421-6958
www.nrndesigns.com

Office Depot
www.officedepot.com

Offray & Son, Inc.
www.offray.com

On The Surface
(847) 675-2520

Once Upon A Scribble
(702) 896-2181
www.onceuponascribble.com

Paper Adventures®
(wholesale only)
(800) 727-0699
www.paperadventures.com

Paper Company, The
(800) 426-8989

Paper Patch®, The
(801) 280-3400
www.paperpatch.com

Papyrus
www.papyrusonline.com

Patchwork Paper Design, Inc.
(480) 515-0537
www.patchworkpaper.com

Pebbles Inc. (wholesale only)
(801) 235-1520
www.pebblesinc.com

Plaid Enterprises, Inc.
(800) 842-2883
www.plaidonline.com

Polyform Products Co.
(847) 427-0020
www.sculpey.com

Postmodern Design LLC
(405) 321-3176

Print Blocks
www.printblocks.com.au

Provo Craft® (wholesale only)
(888) 577-3545
www.provocraft.com

Prym-Dritz Corporation
www.dritz.com

PSX Design™
(800) 782-6748
www.psxdesign.com

Punch Bunch, The
(254) 791-4209
www.thepunchbunch.com

QuicKutz
(888) 702-1146
www.quickutz.com

Ranger Industries, Inc.
(800) 244-2211
www.rangerink.com

Rubba Dub Dub Artist's Stamps
(707) 748-0929
www.artsanctum.com

Rubber Stampede
(800) 423-4135
www.deltacrafts.com

Sakura Hobby Craft
(310) 212-7878
www.sakuracraft.com

Scrapbook Factory Deluxe
(see Nova Development Corporation)

Scrapbook Interiors-SEI, Inc.
(800) 333-3279
www.shopsei.com

Scrap Ease®
(800) 272-3874
www.whatsnewltd.com

Scrap Pagerz™
(435) 645-0696
www.scrappagerz.com

Scrappin' Fools
(702) 564-5101
www.scrappinfools.com

Scrappin' Sports & More
(419) 225-9751
www.scrappinsports.com

ScrapWorks
(713) 842-2547
www.scrapworksllc.com

ScrapYard 329 (wholesale only)
(775) 829-1118
www.scrapyard329.com

Stamp Doctor, The
(208) 286-7644
www.stampdoctor.com

Stampendous!®
(800) 869-0474
www.stampendous.com

Stampin' Up!®
(800) 782-6787
www.stampinup.com

Stamping Station, Inc.
(801) 444-3828
www.stampingstation.com

Staples
www.staples.com

Sweetwater
(800) 359-3094
www.sweetwaterscrapbook.com

Target
www.target.com

Ties That Bind
(505) 762-0295
www.tiesthatbindfiber.com

Treehouse Designs
(877) 372-1109
www.treehouse-designs.com

Tsukineko®, Inc.
(800) 769-6633
www.tsukineko.com

USArtQuest, Inc.
(800) 200-7848
www.usartquest.com

Wal-Mart
www.walmart.com

Westrim® Crafts
(800) 727-2727
www.westrimcrafts.com

Whitman Publishing
no contact info. available

Wilsonart International
(800) 433-3222
www.wilsonart.com

Wordsworth
(719) 282-3495
www.wordsworthstamps.com

Wubie Prints
(888) 256-0107
www.wubieprints.com

Y.L.I.- no contact info. available

Index